Motion Picture Moods

for Pianists and Organists

Motion Picture Moods
for Pianists and Organists

Erno Rapée

ARNO PRESS
A New York Times Company
1974

Reprinted by permission of G. Schirmer, Inc.
Reprinted from a copy in The Museum of Modern Art Library
Library of Congress Catalog Card Number: 70-124035
ISBN 0-405-01635-2

Manufactured in the United States of America

Motion Picture Moods

For

Pianists and Organists

A Rapid-Reference Collection
of Selected Pieces

Arranged By

ERNO RAPÉE

**Adapted to Fifty-Two
Moods and Situations**

G. SCHIRMER, INC., NEW YORK

Printed in the U. S. A.

FOREWORD

AND INSTRUCTIONS FOR THE USE OF THIS MANUAL

In preparing this Motion Picture Manual for Piano and Organ, I tried to create the necessary bridge between the screen and the audience which is created in the larger motion picture houses by the orchestra. If we consider that the theatres of the size and standard of the Capitol Theatre in New York have half a dozen or so musical experts under the direction of the Musical Director working out the music to fit the action on the screen, we realize what a very hard task it must be for any single individual, either at the piano or at the organ, to go through with music selected at random and generally at very short notice, and supply good musical accompaniment to pictures.

This collection is meant to do away with the aforesaid haphazard collection of music and its use for synchronizing pictures. Inasmuch as most pianists or organists in the smaller theatres do not get a chance, or a very poor one, to review the pictures before the public performance, you can readily see the difficulty under which they work with quickly changing scenes, different psychological situations chasing each other, back-shots, close-ups, close-ins, etc., etc. In creating fifty-two divisions and classifications in this Manual, I tried to give the most numbers to those classes of music which are most frequently called upon to synchronize actions on the screen. Let me say here for the information of every man attempting to use this Manual to the best of his advantage that you can't always portray action; one-third of all film footage is used to depict action; another third will show no physical action, but will have, as a preponderance, psychologic situations; the remaining third will neither show action nor suggest psychological situations, but will restrict itself to showing or creating atmosphere or scenery. If it is action that the organist or pianist wants to portray, he will find a sufficient variety of headings in the index to satisfy almost any aspect of his musical taste; should the portrayal of psychological situations be necessary, he will find it under the heading of Love, Horror, Joyfulness, Passion, etc. In the music of 'Nationalties' Chinese and Japanese music has been treated as a unit; the less known national airs of Honduras, Uruguay and Venezuela I enclose only for the rare use in news reels; for Tournaments, Skating, or any exhibition of individual skill where the action is not too fast I advise the use of concert waltzes by Waldteufel, Strauss, etc.; should the action be rather rapid, a galop or lively one-step would be suitable. One-steps and fox-trots have not been included, as most of them are of passing interest and can readily be had in any quantity from all dealers. Under the caption of 'Neutral' you will find seven different numbers which are meant for use in situations where none of the aforesaid three situations are present—that is, where *there is neither action*, nor atmosphere, nor the elements of human temperament present in any noteworthy degree. The music found under the caption 'Sinister' is meant for situations like the presence of the captured enemy, demolishing of a hostile aëroplane or battleship, or for the picturing of anything unsympathetic. The eleven pieces included under the caption 'Parties' will be found suitable also for the portrayal of social gatherings in gardens.

I advise every one trying to get the best use out of this Manual not only to read these instructions carefully, but also to acquaint himself thoroughly with the contents of the whole Manual; only in that way will he derive the benefit I have striven to give every user of this book through the condensing and summing up of my six years' experience in the Motion Picture game.

ERNO RAPÉE.

TABLE OF CONTENTS

		Page
AËROPLANE		
Rondo Capriccioso	Felix Mendelssohn	2
Scherzo	Felix Mendelssohn	3
BAND		
The German Patrol	Richard Eilenberg, Op. 78	5
BATTLE		
Agitato No. 3	Otto Langey	10
Presto agitato (3d movement Moonlight Sonata)	Ludwig van Beethoven, Op. 27, No. 2	13
Allegro di molto e con brio (1st movement from Sonata Op. 13)	Ludwig van Beethoven	17
BIRDS		
Birds	N. Louise Wright, Op. 36, No. 3	21
Papillon (Butterfly)	Edvard Grieg, Op. 43, No. 1	23
Vöglein (Birdling)	Edvard Grieg, Op. 43, No. 4	26
CHATTER		
Presto (last movement from Sonata Op. 10, No. 2)	Ludwig van Beethoven	28
Song without Words (Tarantella)	Felix Mendelssohn, Op. 102, No. 3	29
CHILDREN		
Dickory, dickory, dock (Song)		31
Ding dong bell (Song)		31
Hey, diddle diddle (Song)		32
Humpty Dumpty (Song)		33
Jack and Jill (Song)		34
Mary had a little lamb (Song)		35
Children's Dance	T. Tertius Noble	36
DANCES		
Gavottes:		
Mignon	Ambroise Thomas	39
The Fair Flatterer	Richard Eilenberg, Op. 25	43
Mazurkas:		
La Czarina	Louis Ganne	48
Mazurka	Theodora Dutton, Op. 11, No. 2	51
Minuets:		
Minuet (from Sonata Op. 49, No. 2)	Ludwig van Beethoven	54
Minuet	Luigi Boccherini	58
Polkas:		
Wildfeuer	Johann Strauss, Op. 313	61
Auf freiem Fusse	Johann Strauss, Op. 345	63

Table of Contents

		Page
Valses:		
Tales of the Vienna Wood	Johann Strauss	65
Les Sirènes	Emil Waldteufel	71
Valses Lentes:		
Monte Cristo	Istvan Kotlar	78
April Smile	Maurice Depret, Op. 11	83
Ballroom Whispers (Ballgeflüster)	Louis Gregh, Op. 66	88
Tangos:		
Dengozo (Brazilian)	Ernesto Nazareth	94
Y. . . ¿Como le va? (Argentine)	Joaquin Valverde	98
Marches:		
Exhibition March	Philipp Fahrbach, Jr., Op. 263	102
Standard-bearer March	Philipp Fahrbach, Jr., Op. 192	105
Attack by the Uhlans	Carl Bohm, Op. 213	108
Friedrichs-Marsch	Josef Gungl, Op. 145	114
With the Military	Philipp Fahrbach, Jr.	117
Vienna March	J. Schrammel	120
Rheinland Regiment March	Johann N. Král,	126
DOLL		
The Golden Wedding (La Cinquantaine)	Gabriel-Marie	129
Poupée Valsante	Eduard Poldini	134
FESTIVAL		
Marche Héroïque	Franz Schubert	140
Coronation March	Giacomo Meyerbeer	144
March and Procession of Bacchus (from the Ballet *Sylvia*)	Léo Delibes	148
FIRE-FIGHTING		
Hurry No 2	Otto Langey	151
Agitato No. 2	J. E. Andino	153
Furioso No. 3	Otto Langey	155
Card Trio (from the opera *Carmen*)	Georges Bizet	157
From the Ballet-Suite *Salammbô*	H. Arends	159
FUNERAL		
Marche Funèbre (from Sonata Op. 35)	Frédéric Chopin	160
Andante Pathétique No. 1	Robert Schumann	161
Funeral March (Song without Words)	Felix Mendelssohn, Op. 62, No. 3	163
GROTESQUE		
Misterioso No. 1	Otto Langey	165
Tanz aus Jölster (Dance from Jölster)	Edvard Grieg, Op. 17, No. 5	167
GRUESOME		
Misterioso Infernale	Gaston Borch	169
Misterioso No. 2	Adolf Minot	171
Andante molto sostenuto (from *Phèdre* overture)	Jules Massenet	173

Table of Contents

		PAGE
HORROR		
ABDUCTION OF THE BRIDE (2d Peer Gynt Suite)	Edvard Grieg, Op. 55	173
HUMOROUS		
HUMORESQUE	P. I. Tschaikowsky, Op. 10, No. 2	174
CURIOUS STORY (Kuriose Geschichte)	Stephen Heller	178
HUMORESQUE	Edvard Grieg, Op. 6, No. 3	180
STABBE-LAATEN (Humoristic Dance)	Edvard Grieg, Op. 17, No. 18	181
LE COUCOU	Anton Arensky, Op. 34, No. 2	183
HUNTING		
JAGDLIED (Hunting-Song)	Robert Schumann, Op. 82	186
JAGD-FANFARE (Hunter's Call)	Hugo Reinhold, Op. 39	190
JÄGERLIEDCHEN (Hunting-Song)	Robert Schumann	191
THE HUNTER'S HORN	Anton Schmoll, Op. 50	192
IMPATIENCE		
IMPATIENCE (Song without Words)	Louis Gregh	194
UNTIRING SEARCH	Heinrich Stiehl, Op. 64, No. 4	197
SONG WITHOUT WORDS (Homeless)	Felix Mendelssohn, Op. 102, No. 1	199
JOYFULNESS or HAPPINESS		
HAPPY WANDERER	Adolf Jensen	202
A LA POLKA	Zdenko Fibich, Op. 41, No. 10	206
LOVE-THEMES		
THE OLD MOTHER	Anton Dvořák	209
ROMANCE	Frederick A. Williams, Op. 88	211
VALSE	Johannes Brahms	215
POEM	Zdenko Fibich	217
CAVATINA	Joachim Raff	219
LOVE-SONG	Rudolf Friml, Op. 85 bis, No. 3	223
MELODY	Anton Rubinstein, Op. 3, No. 1	226
CHANT D'AMOUR (Love-Song)	Ignace J. Paderewski, Op. 10, No. 2	229
LULLABIES		
BERCEUSE	Alexander Iljinsky, Op. 13	231
LULLABY	N. Louise Wright, Op. 30	233
BERCEUSE	Edvard Grieg, Op. 38, No. 1	235
SERENADE	Marian Sokolowski, Op. 4, No. 3	238
MISTERIOSO		
ZUG DER ZWERGE (March of the Dwarfs)	Edvard Grieg, Op. 54, No. 3	242
ALLEGRO MISTERIOSO NOTTURNO	Gaston Borch	244
AGITATO MISTERIOSO	Otto Langey	246
THE ERL-KING (Le Roi des Aulnes)	Franz Schubert	248
MONOTONY		
PRELUDE	Frédéric Chopin	250
BÅDNLÅT (Cradle-Song)	Edvard Grieg, Op. 66, No. 15	252

Table of Contents

		PAGE
MUSIC-BOX		
Music-Box	Rudolf Friml, Op. 69	254
Une Tabatière à Musique (Valse-Badinage)	Anatole Liadow, Op. 32	257
Klokkeklang (Ringing Bells)	Edvard Grieg, Op. 54, No. 6	259
NATIONAL		
United States of America:		
Star-Spangled Banner (National Hymn)	John Stafford Smith	261
America (My country, 'tis of thee)	Henry Carey	262
Hail Columbia	Patriotic Air	262
The Red, White and Blue—Columbia, the Gem of the Ocean	Patriotic Air	264
The Battle-Cry of Freedom (Song)	George F. Root	265
Battle Hymn of the Republic (Song)	Patriotic Air	267
Tramp! tramp! tramp! (Song)	Patriotic Air	269
Yankee Doodle (Song)	Patriotic Air	271
Bugle-Calls:		
Reveille	Arthur Tomlinson	273
Taps	Arthur Tomlinson	274
Adjutant's Call	Arthur Tomlinson	275
The General's March	Arthur Tomlinson	276
Assembly March	Arthur Tomlinson	277
To the Colors	Arthur Tomlinson	277
Southern:		
Southwestern Idyl	Irénée Bergé	279
Dixie-Land (Southern Air)	Dan Emmet	281
My Old Kentucky Home (Folk-song)	Stephen C. Foster	282
Old Folks at Home (Swanee River)	Stephen C. Foster	283
Plantation Melody	Arthur Farwell	284
College:		
College Songs March	Thomas G. Shepard	285
Alma Mater		289
Fair Harvard		290
Gaudeamus		290
Upidee		291
We won't go home till morning		291
Sea-Songs:		
Nancy Lee (Song)	Stephen Adams	292
Rocked in the Cradle of the Deep (Song)	Joseph P. Knight	295
Christmas Songs:		
Jingle Bells		299
Hark! the herald angels sing	Felix Mendelssohn	300
Adeste Fideles	John Reading	301
Holy Night	Franz Gruber	302
Old Ballads:		
Sally in Our Alley	Henry Carey	303
Home, Sweet Home	H. R. Bishop	304
Love's Old, Sweet Song	J. L. Molloy	305
Robin Adair		306
Alice, where art thou?	J. Ascher	307
Listen to the mocking-bird	Alice Hawthorne	309
When you and I were young, Maggie	J. A. Butterfield	310

Table of Contents

		PAGE
Argentine Republic		
OID, MORTALES, EL GRITO SAGRADO	National Hymn	311
Australia		
THERE IS A LAND WHERE SUMMER SKIES	Patriotic Air	314
Austria		
O DU MEIN ÖSTERREICH	Patriotic Air	315
Bohemia		
BOHEMIA	Patriotic Air	316
Belgium		
LA BRABANÇONNE	National Hymn	317
Brazil		
NATIONAL HYMN		318
Bulgaria		
NATIONAL HYMN		319
Canada		
THE MAPLE-LEAF FOR EVER	Patriotic Song	320
VIVE LA CANADIENNE	Patriotic Song	321
Chili		
DULCE PATRIA	National Song	322
China		
NATIONAL HYMN		324, 330
United States of Columbia		
NATIONAL HYMN		324
Costa Rica		
DE LA PATRIA	National Song	326
Cuba		
LA BAYAMESA	National Song	327
DANZAS Nos. I-II (from Six Cuban Dances)	Ignacio Cervantes	328
China and Japan		
KIMYGAYO	Japanese Natl. Hymn	330
CHINESE-JAPANESE	Otto Langey	331
IN A CHINESE TEA-ROOM	Otto Langey, Op. 158, No. 2	333
CHINESE LULLABY (*East is West*) (Song)	Robert H. Bowers	338
FUJI-KO (Japanese Intermezzo)	Harry Rowe Shelley	340
Denmark		
NATIONAL HYMN		344
England		
GOD SAVE THE KING	Henry Carey	345
RULE, BRITANNIA	Patriotic Air	345
DRINK TO ME ONLY WITH THINE EYES (Song)	Old English Air	346
France		
LA MARSEILLAISE	National Hymn	349
PARTANT POUR LA SYRIE	Patriotic Air	350
CHANT DU DÉPART	Patriotic Air	351
MOURIR POUR LA PATRIE	Patriotic Air	352

Table of Contents

		PAGE
Germany		
DIE WACHT AM RHEIN	National Hymn	353
STIMMT AN MIT HELLEM, HOHEN KLANG	National Song	353
Greece		
NATIONAL HYMN		354
Hawaii		
HAWAII POUOI	National Hymn	354
OLOHA, OE	National Song	355
Holland		
MIJN NEÊRLANDSCH BLOED	National Hymn	356
Honduras		
DIOS SALVE A HONDURAS	National Song	357
Hungary		
NATIONAL SONG		358
RÁKÓCZY MARCH	Patriotic Air	359
Gipsy		
SLAVIC DANCE	Anton Dvořák, Op. 72	361
Indian (West)		
INDIAN AGITATO	Otto Langey	367
INDIAN WAR-DANCE	Irénée Bergé	369
INDIAN WAR-DANCE	Gaston Borch	371
SUN-DANCE	Lily Strickland	373
DANCE OF THE YOUNG MAIDENS	Lily Strickland	377
Irish		
GARRY OWEN		381
COLLEGE HORNPIPE		382
FISCHER'S HORNPIPE		382
KILLARNEY		383
THE WEARING O' THE GREEN	Patriotic Air	384
SAINT PATRICK'S DAY	National Song	385
Italy		
FANFARE E MARCIA REALE	National Hymn	386
GARIBALDI HYMN	Patriotic Air	389
MARIA, MARÌ! (Marie, ah Marie!) (Song)	Eduardo Di Capua	391
'O SOLE MIO (My Sunshine) (Song)	Eduardo Di Capua	394
VENETIAN BOAT-SONG	Felix Mendelssohn, Op. 30, No. 6	396
BARCAROLLE (from *Tales of Hoffmann*)	Jacques Offenbach	398
TARENTELLE	Théodore Lack, Op. 20	400
Mexico		
LA GOLANDRINA	National Song	406
Norwegian and Swedish		
SÖNNER AF NORGE	Norwegian Natl. Song	408
WALZER	Edvard Grieg, Op. 12, No. 2	409
NORWEGISCH (Norwegian Melody)	Edvard Grieg, Op. 12, No. 6	411
NORWEGIAN DANCE	Edvard Grieg, Op. 35, No. 2	413
SWEDISH WEDDING MARCH (Idylle aus der Hochzeit zu Wulfsberg)	August Söderman, Op. 12	416

Table of Contents

		Page
Poland		
Poland's not yet dead in slavery	Patriotic Air	419
Krakowiak (Polonaise)	Emil Mlynarski, Op. 5, No. 1	420
Portugal		
Marcia	National Hymn	423
Roumania		
Traesca Regele	National Hymn	424
Russia		
The Hymn of Free Russia (Gimn svobodnoi Rossii) (Song)	Alexandre Gretchaninoff	425
Cossack Lullaby	J. Jiránek	429
Russian Dance	Rudolf Friml, Op. 83, No. 4	431
Scotland		
Auld Lang Syne	Folk-song	439
The Campbells are coming	National Song	440
The Bluebells of Scotland	National Song	440
Annie Laurie	Folk-song	441
Scots, wha hae wi' Wallace bled	National Song	442
Comin' Through the Rye	Folk-song	443
Serbia		
Srpska Narodna Himna (Song)	National Hymn	444
Spain		
Himno de Riego	National Hymn	446
Spanish Dance No. 1	Moritz Moszkowski	447
Spanish Dance No. 2	Moritz Moszkowski	450
Juanita (Song)	Spanish Ballad	453
Estudiantina (Valses)	Emil Waldteufel	455
Uruguay		
National Hymn		463
Venezuela		
Gloria al bravo pueblo	National Hymn	465
Wales		
Men of Harlech	National Song	466
NEUTRAL		
Radiance	Gatty Sellars	467
The Lotus Lake	Theodora Dutton	471
Albumblatt (Album-Leaf)	Edvard Grieg, Op. 12, No. 7	474
Arabesque	Basile Wrangell, Op. 1, No. 3	476
Moment Musical No. 1	Franz Schubert, Op. 94	479
Moment Musical No. 3	Franz Schubert, Op. 94	483
Chant sans Paroles	Rudolf Friml, Op. 49	485
ORGIES		
L'Arlésienne Suite, 4th movement	Georges Bizet	487
L'Automne et l'Hiver (Autumn and Winter)	Alexandre Glazounoff	494

Table of Contents

		Page
ORIENTAL		
Among the Arabs	Otto Langey, Op. 158, No. 1	496
Morris Dance	T. Tertius Noble	501
Vers l'Oasis (In Sight of the Oasis)	Maurice Baron	506
Arab Dance	Edvard Grieg	510
L'Arlésienne Suite, 1st movement	Georges Bizet	519
PARTIES		
Vanity (Caprice)	Ralph C. Jackson	523
Idilio	Théodore Lack, Op. 134	527
Scarf Dance (Scène de Ballet)	Cécile Chaminade	530
Souvenir	Franz Drdla	533
Pizzicati (from the Ballet *Sylvia*)	Léo Delibes	538
Sérénade Badine	Gabriel-Marie	542
Serenata	Moritz Moszkowski, Op. 15, No. 1	547
Ladies' Faces, Ribbons and Laces (Old-time Gavotte)	Eugene Wyatt	550
Spring Song (Song without Words)	Felix Mendelssohn, Op. 62, No. 6	553
Chant sans Paroles (Song without Words)	P. I. Tschaikowsky	557
Salut d'Amour (Love's Greeting)	Edward Elgar, Op. 12	560
PASTORALE		
Morgenstimmung (Morning Mood)	Edvard Grieg, Op. 46, No. 1	564
Le Carillon (4th movement l'Arlésienne Suite)	Georges Bizet	568
Pastorale (1st movement l'Arlésienne Suite No. 2)	Georges Bizet	570
PASSION		
Valzer Appassionato	Theodora Dutton	571
Song without Words (Lost Happiness)	Felix Mendelssohn, Op. 38, No. 2	577
Song without Words (Homeless)	Felix Mendelssohn, Op. 102, No. 1	579
An den Frühling (To Spring)	Edvard Grieg, Op. 43, No. 6	582
PULSATING		
Repose (Song without Words)	Louis Gregh, Op. 53	587
QUIETUDE and PURITY		
Adagio (3d movement l'Arlésienne Suite)	Georges Bizet	591
Le Soir (Eventide)	Ludwig Schytte, Op. 12, No. 3	592
Song without Words (Faith)	Felix Mendelssohn, Op. 102, No. 6	594
Träumerei	Robert Schumann, Op. 15, No. 7	596
Serenade	Ole Olsen	597
RACE		
Allegro No. 1	Adolf Minot	599
Galop (Leichtes Blut)	Johann Strauss, Op. 319	601
Galop (Die Bajadère)	Johann Strauss, Op. 351	603
Galop (Cascaden)	H. Herrmann, Op. 24	605
RAILROAD		
The Mill (Die Mühle)	Adolf Jensen	608
Spinning-Song (from *The Flying Dutchman*)	Richard Wagner	612

Table of Contents

		Page
RELIGIOSO		
Largo	G. F. Händel	616
The Old Hundredth (Song)	L. Bourgeois	619
Onward, Christian Soldiers (Song)	Arthur S. Sullivan	619
Lead, Kindly Light	Hymn	620
SADNESS		
Romance	H. Frommel	621
Sonata quasi una Fantasia (1st movement)	Ludwig van Beethoven, Op. 27, No. 2	625
Prelude	Frédéric Chopin, Op. 28, No. 4	629
Prelude	Frédéric Chopin, Op. 28, No. 20	630
Élégie	Edvard Grieg, Op. 47	631
Berceuse	Armas Järnefelt	633
Åse's Death	Edvard Grieg, Op. 46, No. 2	636
Romance	Anton Rubinstein, Op. 44, No. 1	638
Chanson Triste	P. I. Tschaikowsky, Op. 40, No. 2	640
Album-Leaf	L. Birkedal-Barfod, from Op. 7	642
Andante Patetico e Doloroso	Gaston Borch	644
Pathetic Andante No. 1	Otto Langey	646
Herzwunden (Heart-Sores)	Edvard Grieg, Op. 34, No. 1	647
Mélodie (Élégie)	Jules Massenet, Op. 10	649
SEA and STORM		
In der Halle des Bergkönigs (In the Hall of the Mountain King)	Edvard Grieg, Op. 46, No. 4	651
Stormy Evening on the Coast (Peer Gynt's Home-coming)	Edvard Grieg	655
SINISTER		
Coriolan Overture	Ludwig van Beethoven	663
WESTERN		
Western Allegro	Edward Falck	665
Western Allegro	Hugo Riesenfeld	667
Western Scene	Irénée Bergé	669
WEDDING		
Hochzeit-Marsch (Wedding March)	Felix Mendelssohn	671
Hochzeit-Marsch (Wedding March, from *Lohengrin*)	Richard Wagner	672
O promise me	Reginald de Koven	673

Motion Picture Moods

Rondo Capriccioso
Presto (♩. = 104)
F. Mendelssohn
pp
leggiero
Ped.
dim.
pp
D C
1914

Scherzo

F. Mendelssohn

10830
31381

pp staccato.
p
p
f
p
f
f
p
p
pp
D. C.

The German Patrol

Edited by Andor Pintér

Richard Eilenberg. Op.78

Tempo di Marcia

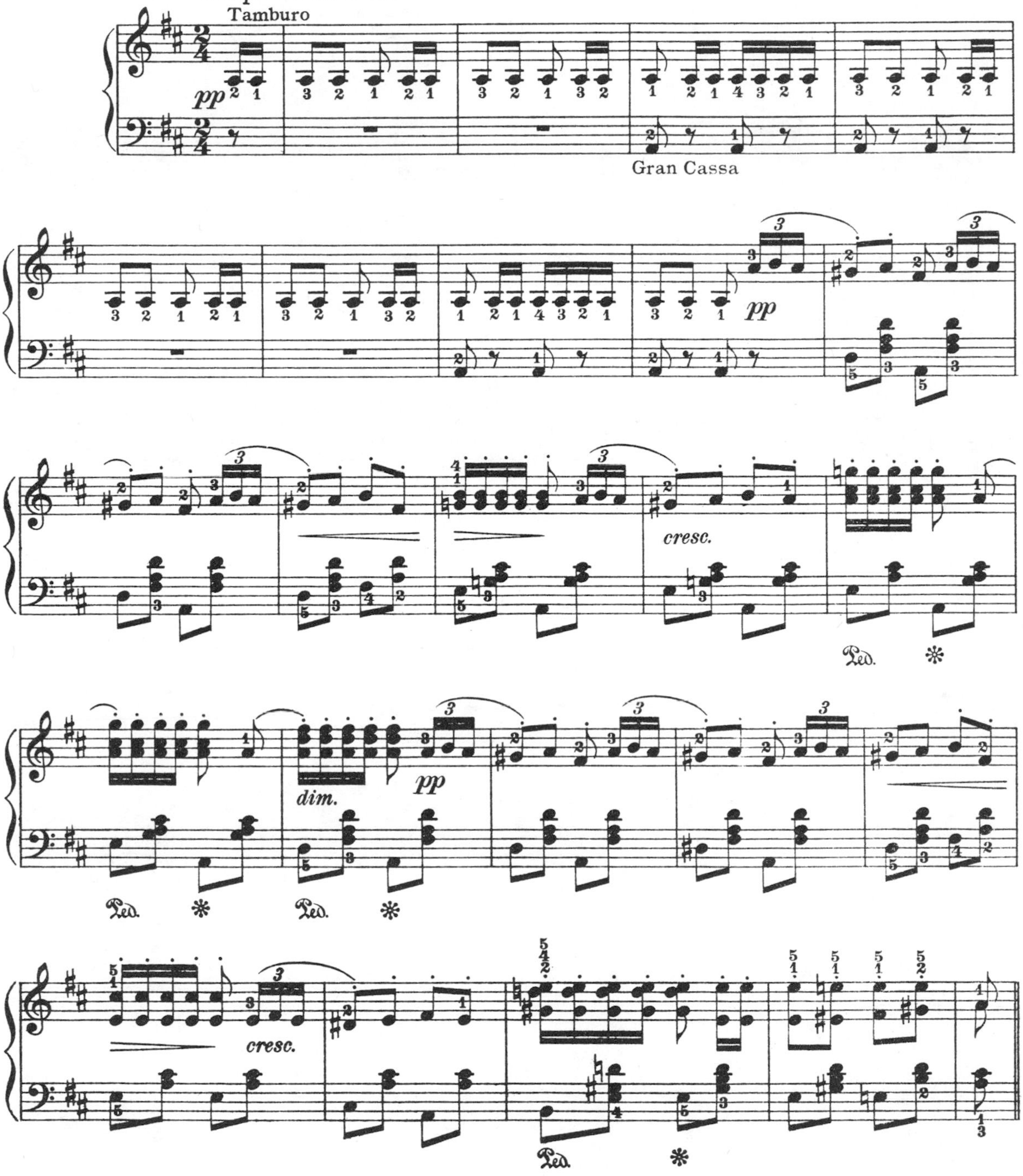

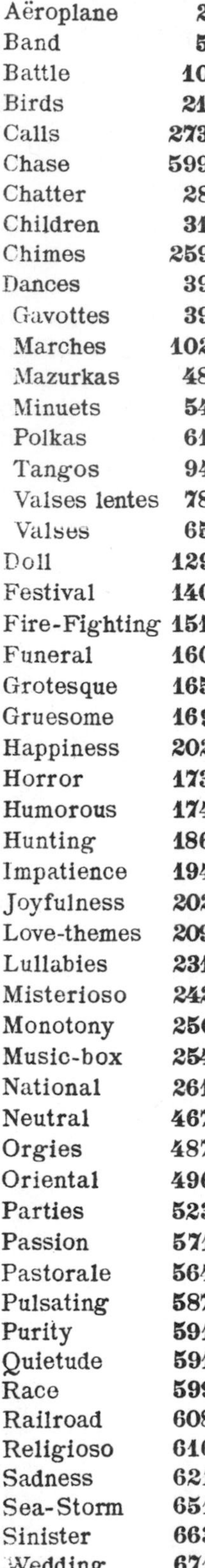

cresc.
Ped.

mf
f
mf
f
mf
f
ff
con fuoco
ff
Ped.

ff
Ped. Ped. Ped. Ped.
D. C.

Agitato No. 3

(Suitable for gruesome or infernal scenes, witches, *etc.*)

Otto Langey

Allegro agitato

mf

f

cresc.
mf
ff
mf
cresc.
ff
8
mf
8

1.
2.
sfz
Presto
ff
1.
D. C.
CODA
2.
ff
sffz

Third Movement
from
Sonata Op. 27, No. 2

L. van Beethoven

Presto agitato. (𝅗𝅥 = 88.)

a) M.T. b)

p sf p Ped. ✲ dim. cresc. ten. lunga. f

11617

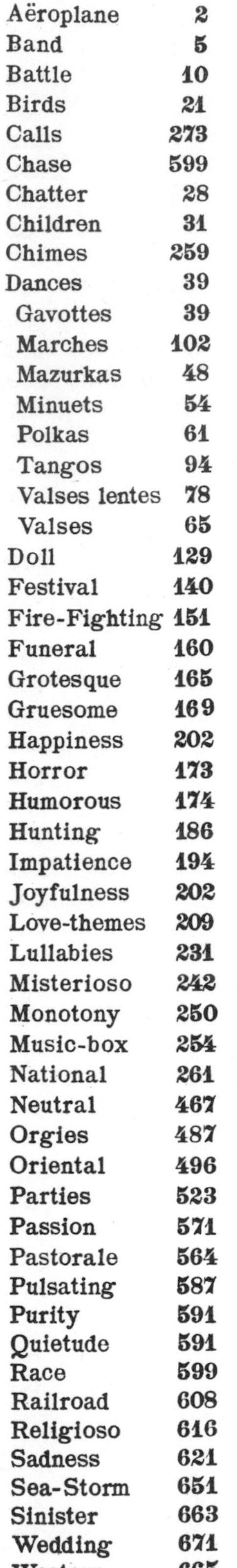

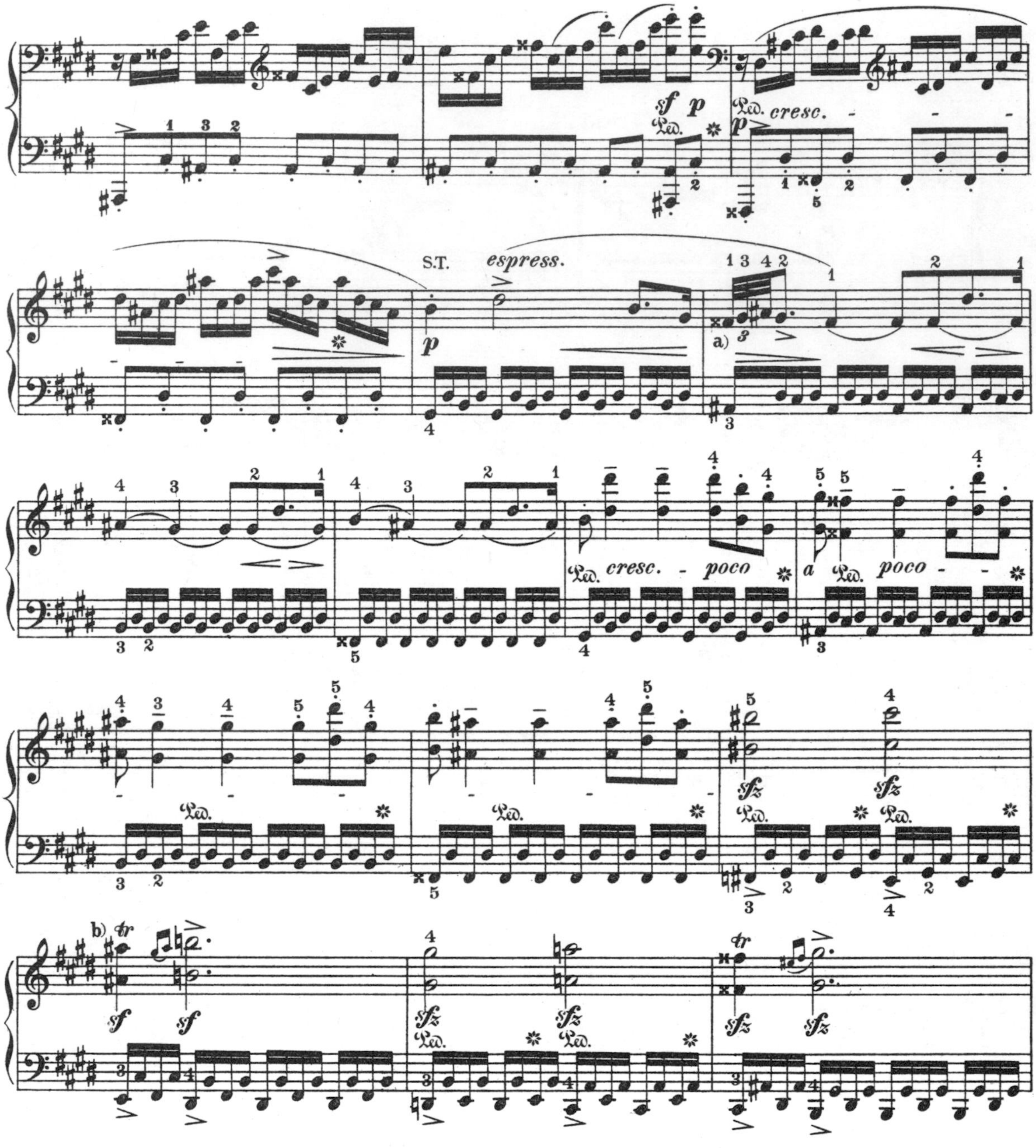

ten.
cresc.
agitato.
Cl.T.I.
a)
b)
p cresc.

sf
simile.
cresc.
decresc.
Cl. T. II.
51
non troppo legato
R. (Tr.)
cresc.

First Movement

from

Sonata Op. 13

L. van Beethoven

p cresc.
sf
p cresc.
sf
p cresc.
sf
sf
sf
sf
poco ritenuto.
a tempo.
S.T.
marcato,
a) ma piano.
p
mfp
ten.
b)
c)
mf
tenuto sempre.

a) These first 4 measures are to be played without the least retardation, yet very quietly, and with no accentuation of the accompaniment.

11611
31381

cresc.
R.(Tr.)
più f

Birds
from
In Springtime

N. Louise Wright. Op.36, No 3

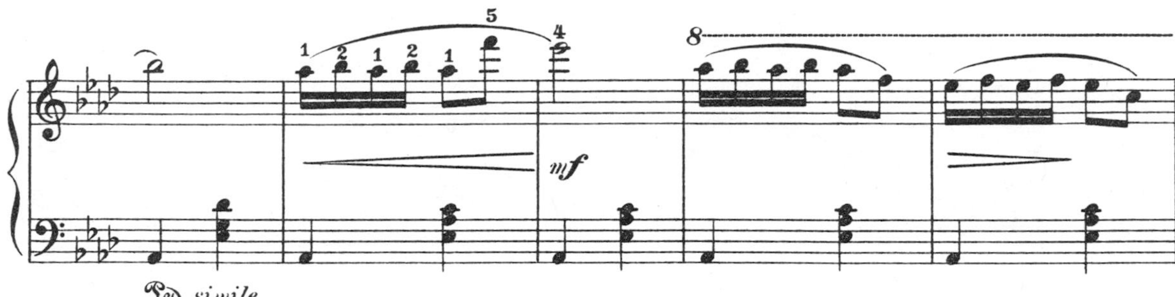

mf
mp
mf
mp
cresc.
Ped.
Ped.

Papillon

(Butterfly)

Revised and fingered by
Wm. Scharfenberg

Edvard Grieg. Op. 43, No. 1

Allegro grazioso. (♩ = 132)

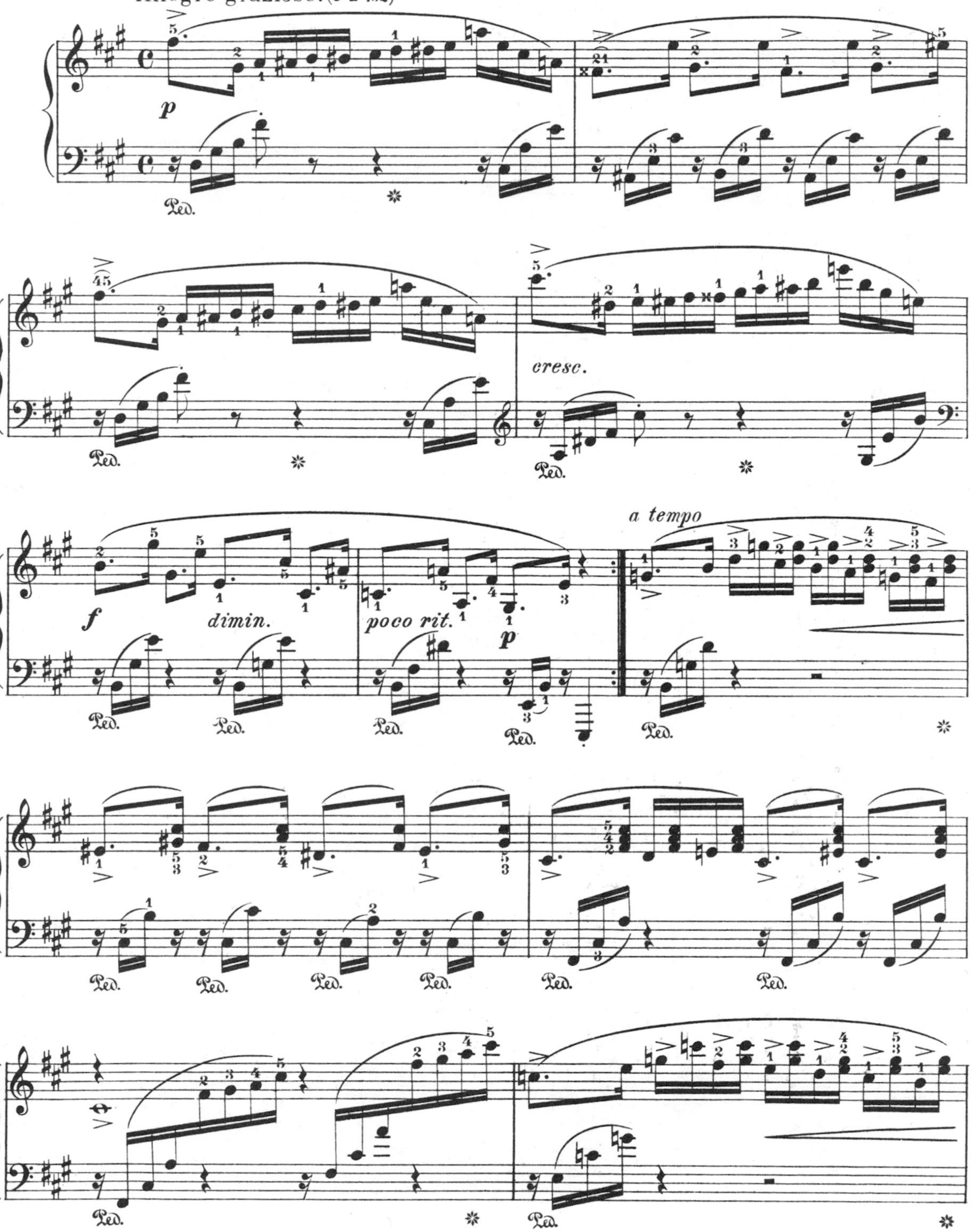

p *cresc.* *f* *dimin.* *poco rit.* *p* *a tempo*

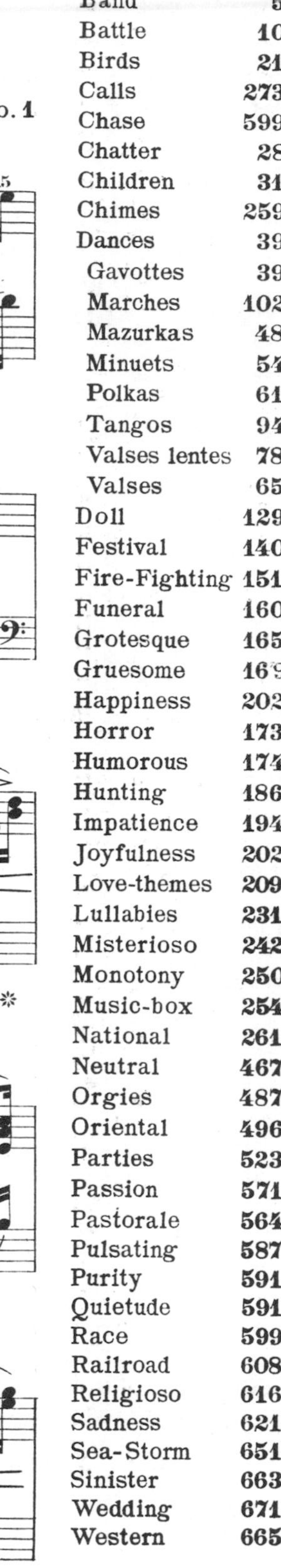

una corda
pp
ritard.
a tempo
dolce
cresc. poco a poco
con moto e poco stretto
tre corde
f
dimin.
p

Ped.
pp una corda
ritard.
a tempo
dolce
cresc. poco a poco e
poco stretto
tre corde
f
ffz
dimin. e rit.
p
pp

Vöglein

(Birdling)

Edited and fingered by
Louis Oesterle

Edvard Grieg. Op. 43, No. 4

15543

cresc.
f
p
pp
ppp
poco ritar - - dan - - - do
Ped.

Last Movement
from
Sonata Op. 10, No. 2

L. van Beethoven

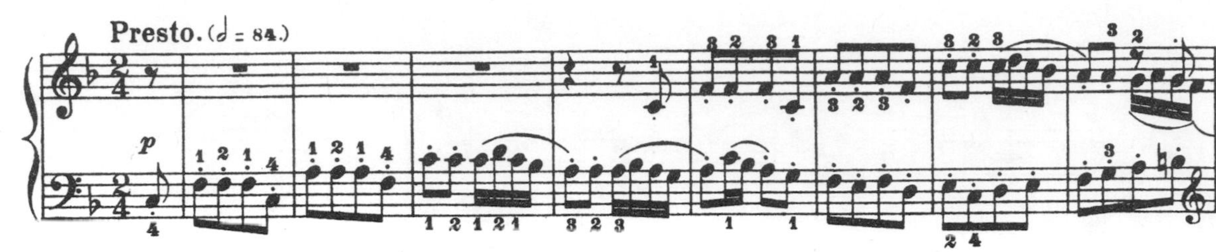

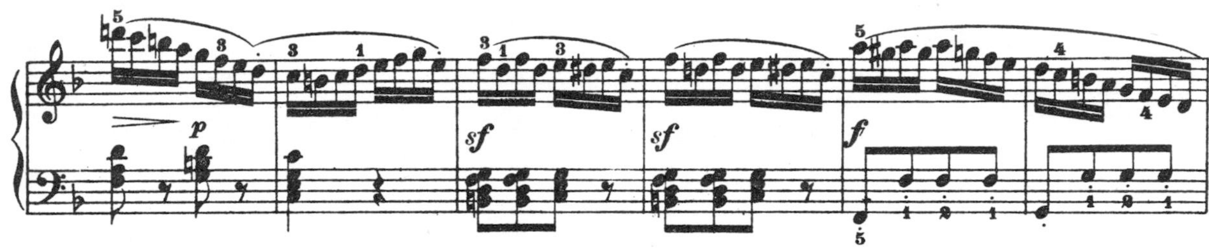

Song without Words
Presto
F. Mendelssohn. Op. 102, No. 3
p
cresc.
f
f
sf
sf
dimin.
Aëroplane 2
Band 5
Battle 10
Birds 21
Calls 273
Chase 599
Chatter 28
Children 31
Chimes 259
Dances 39
Gavottes 39
Marches 102
Mazurkas 48
Minuets 54
Polkas 61
Tangos 94
Valses lentes 78
Valses 65
Doll 129
Festival 140
Fire-Fighting 151
Funeral 160
Grotesque 165
Gruesome 169
Happiness 202
Horror 173
Humorous 174
Hunting 186
Impatience 194
Joyfulness 202
Love-themes 209
Lullabies 231
Misterioso 242
Monotony 250
Music-box 254
National 261
Neutral 467
Orgies 487
Oriental 496
Parties 523
Passion 571
Pastorale 564
Pulsating 587
Purity 591
Quietude 591
Race 599
Railroad 608
Religioso 616
Sadness 621
Sea-Storm 651
Sinister 663
Wedding 671
Western 665

sempre stacc.
p
1.
2.
sempre stacc.
sf
dimin. poco a poco
p
dimin.
pp

Dickory, dickory, dock

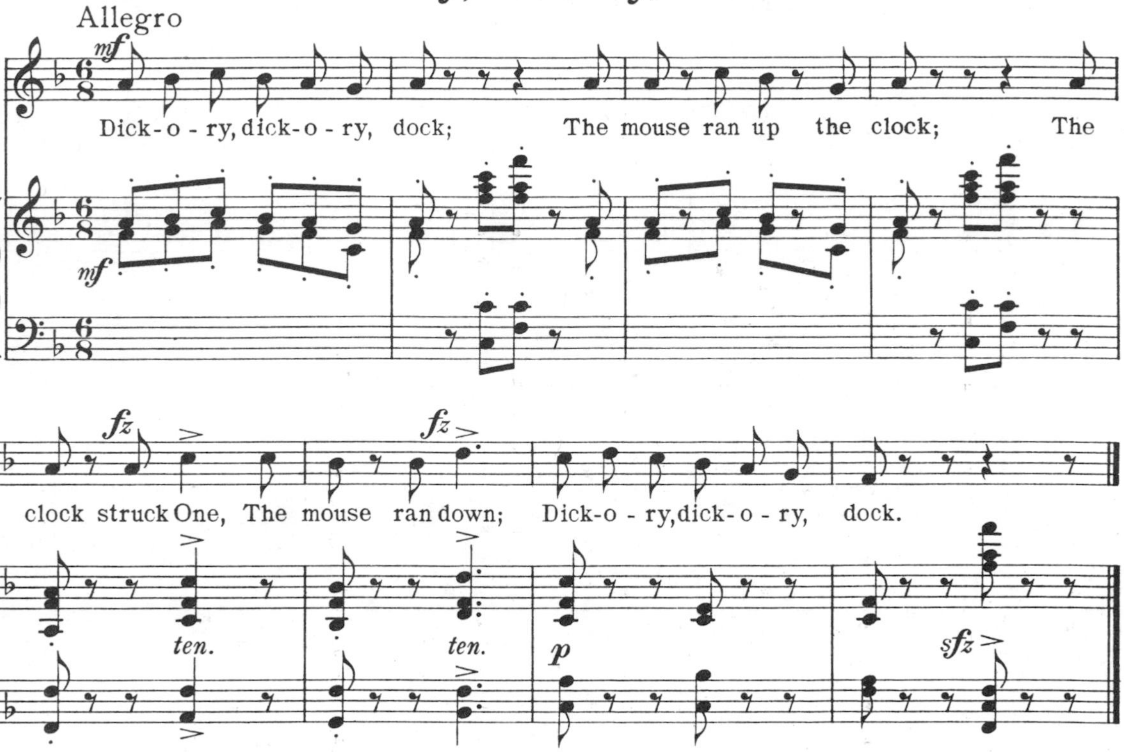

Allegro

Dick-o-ry, dick-o-ry, dock; The mouse ran up the clock; The clock struck One, The mouse ran down; Dick-o-ry, dick-o-ry, dock.

Ding dong bell

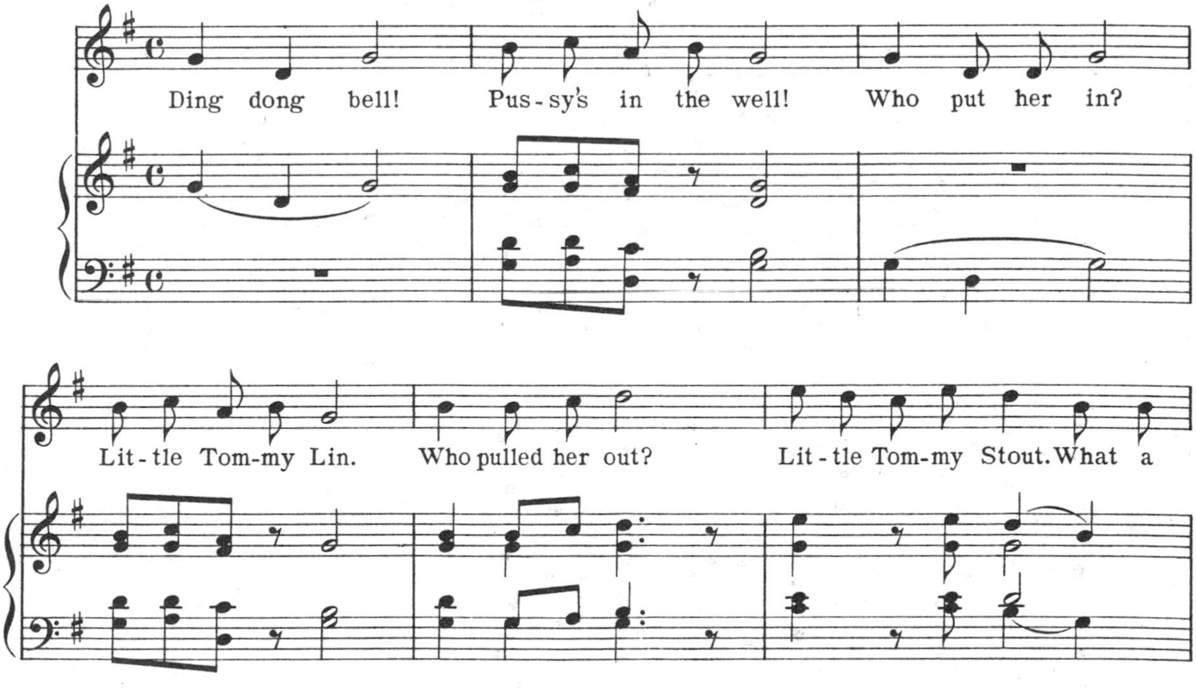

Ding dong bell! Pus-sy's in the well! Who put her in? Lit-tle Tom-my Lin. Who pulled her out? Lit-tle Tom-my Stout. What a

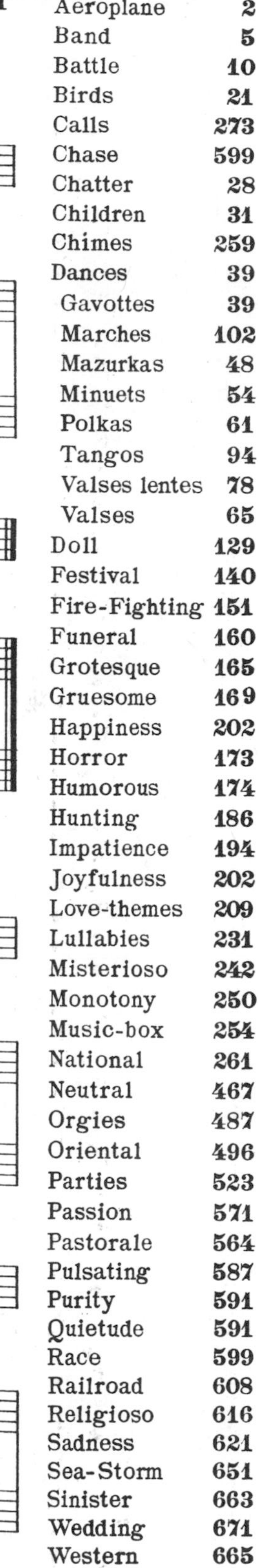

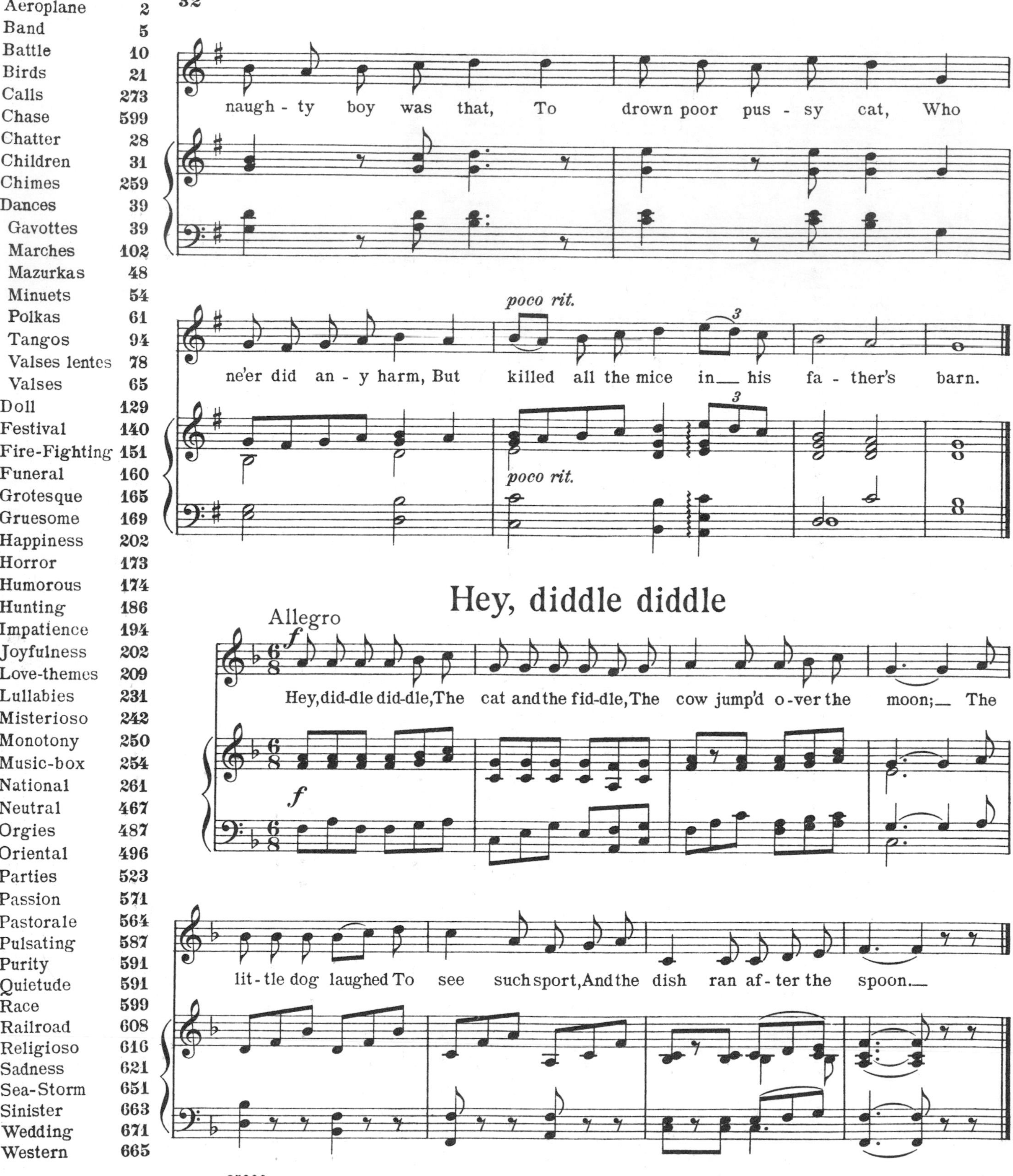

Hey, diddle diddle

Humpty Dumpty

Jack and Jill

Mary had a little lamb

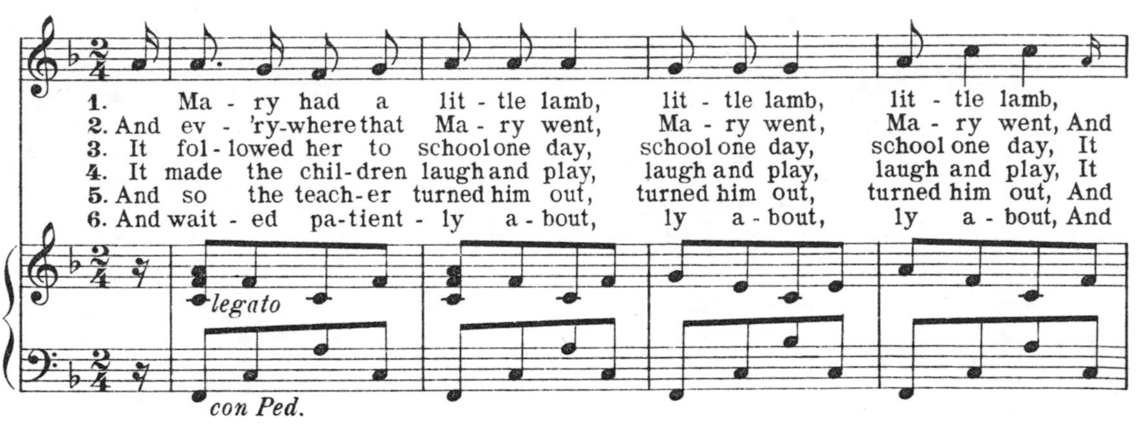

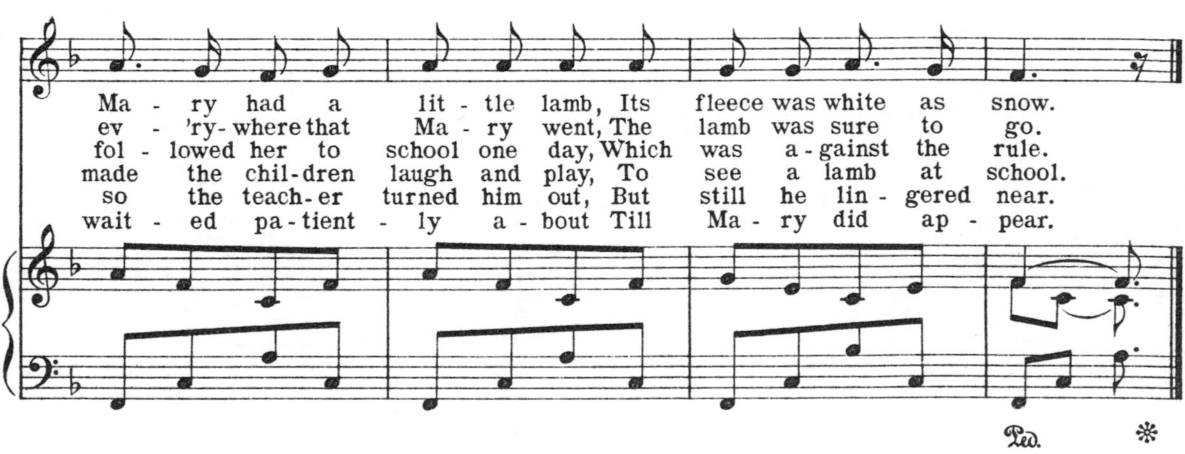

Children's Dance

T. T. Noble

21651
31881

mf
f
ff
mf

ff
mf
f
f
D.C. al Fine

Gavotte

de l'opéra

Mignon

Revised and fingered by
Wm Scharfenberg

A. Thomas
Transcribed by A. Bazille

Allegretto

ff ff ff p pp tr tr

tr
tr
Ped.
Ped.
pp

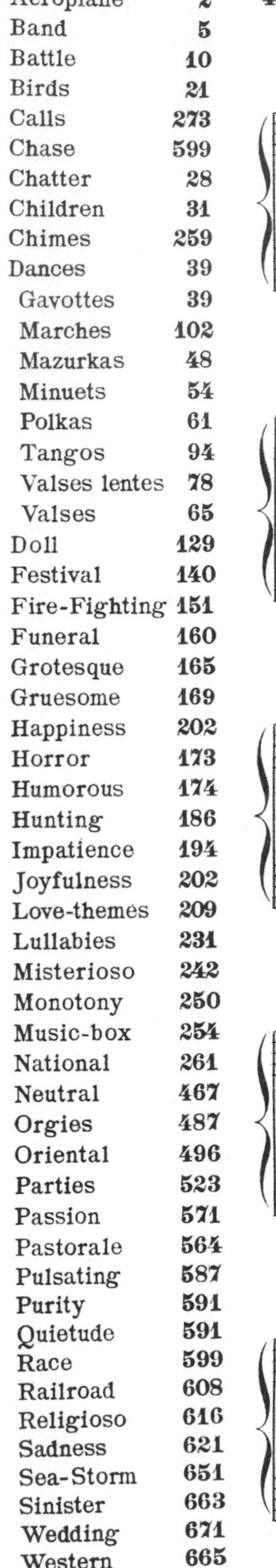

The Fair Flatterer

R. Eilenberg. Op. 25

cresc.
p
p
f
dim.

pp
ff
p
marcato
marcato
ff

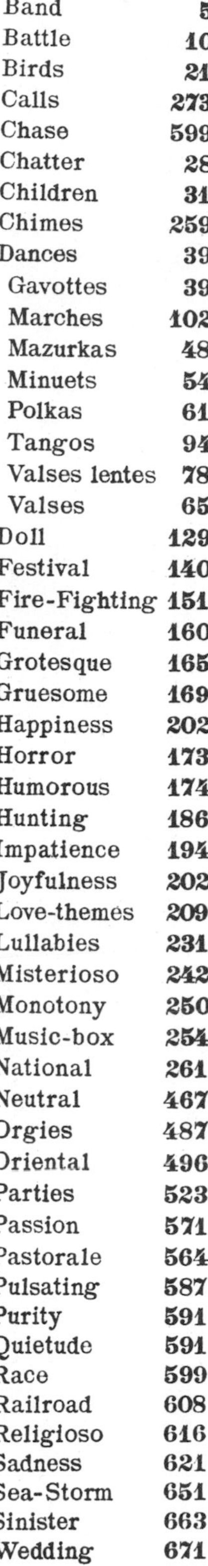

p

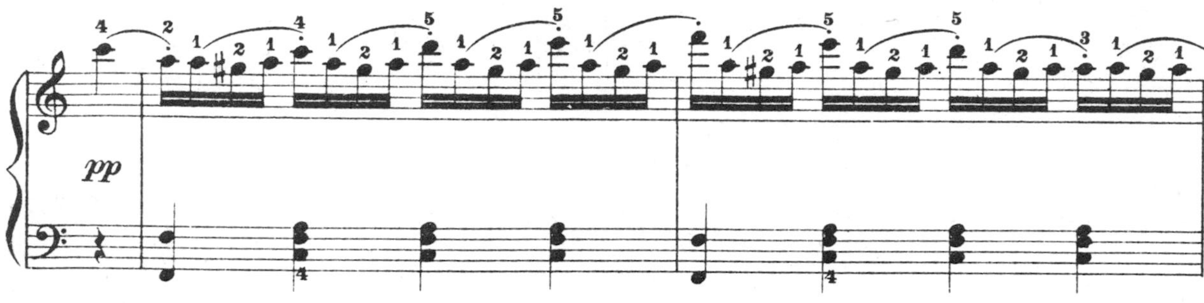
pp

pp

D. C.

La Czarina
Mazurka
ben marcato
L. Ganne
ff
f Trumpets.
simile
ff (tutti.)
mf
allarg.
a tempo
f
ff
p
allarg
a tempo
tr

Trumpets
simile
ff (tutti.)
Accompaniment very lightly (ad lib.)
Trio
sf

ff
mf
ff
mf cresc.
f
1
2
mf
D. C.

Mazurka

Theodora Dutton. Op.11, No.1

Con moto

27838 c
31381

sempre con moto
mp espressivo
cresc.
Ped.
Ped.
simile
un poco rit.
p cresc. poco a poco
dim. poco a poco
rit. molto
a tempo
p espressivo

mp
sf
mf cresc.
sf
poco a poco
sf
mf cresc.
sf
ff
ff
f
ff
un poco rit.
ff

Minuet

from

Sonata Op. 49, No. 2

cresc.
f
p
p
poco rit.
pp

a tempo.
p
cresc.
mp
cresc.
f
f
p
p
p
cresc.
f dimin.

pp
p
cresc.
mp
cresc.
Coda.
f
p
mf
cresc.
f
poco rit.
pp

Minuet

Edited and fingered by
Louis Oesterle

Luigi Boccherini

TRIO
p
p dolce e leggiero
ben sostenuto
mf
mf
f
p
3428

f
p
cresc.
tr
f
p
f
p
allargando
cresc.
tr
f

Wildfeuer
Polka

Johann Strauss. Op. 313

Trio.
1.
2.
Dal 𝄋 al segno 𝄌, poi Coda.
Coda.

Auf freiem Fusse

Polka

Johann Strauss. Op. 345

Trio.
Dal 𝄋 al segno Φ, poi Coda
Φ Coda.

Tales of the Vienna Wood

Johann Strauss

1.
2.
pp
mf
f
1.
2.
Ending.
3.
p
pp
1.
2.
Ending.
p
mf
Fine.
mf
f
1.
2.
mf
f
f
p
D. S.

13522
31384

pp
1.
2.
Ending.
mf
mf
f
Fine.
mf
fz
f
mf
D. S.
Coda.
p
cresc.
f

tr
p
Ped.
pp un poco ritenuto
a tempo
cresc.
f

pp
mf
f
fz
ff
(N. B. When for dancing leave out from A to B.)
A
una corda
pp rit.
pp molto
rit.
p
ritard.
B a tempo.
Ped.
f tremolo

Les Sirènes
Valse
E. Waldteufel
1.
p
f

con fuoco
2.
ff
1.
2.
con espressione
p
cresc.
dim.
f grandioso

3.
scherzando
p
8
poco a poco cresc.
f
1.
2.
Più mosso.
stringendo
ff

grandioso
4.
mf
p
f
p
scherzando
f
1.
2.

Coda.
f
p
f
p
ff
p
p
1.
2.
p
f
1.
p
2.
p
mf

cresc
ff
sonore.
f
risoluto

energico
fff

Monte Cristo

Celebrated Hungarian Waltz

Istvan Kotlar

15283

Printed in the U. S. A.

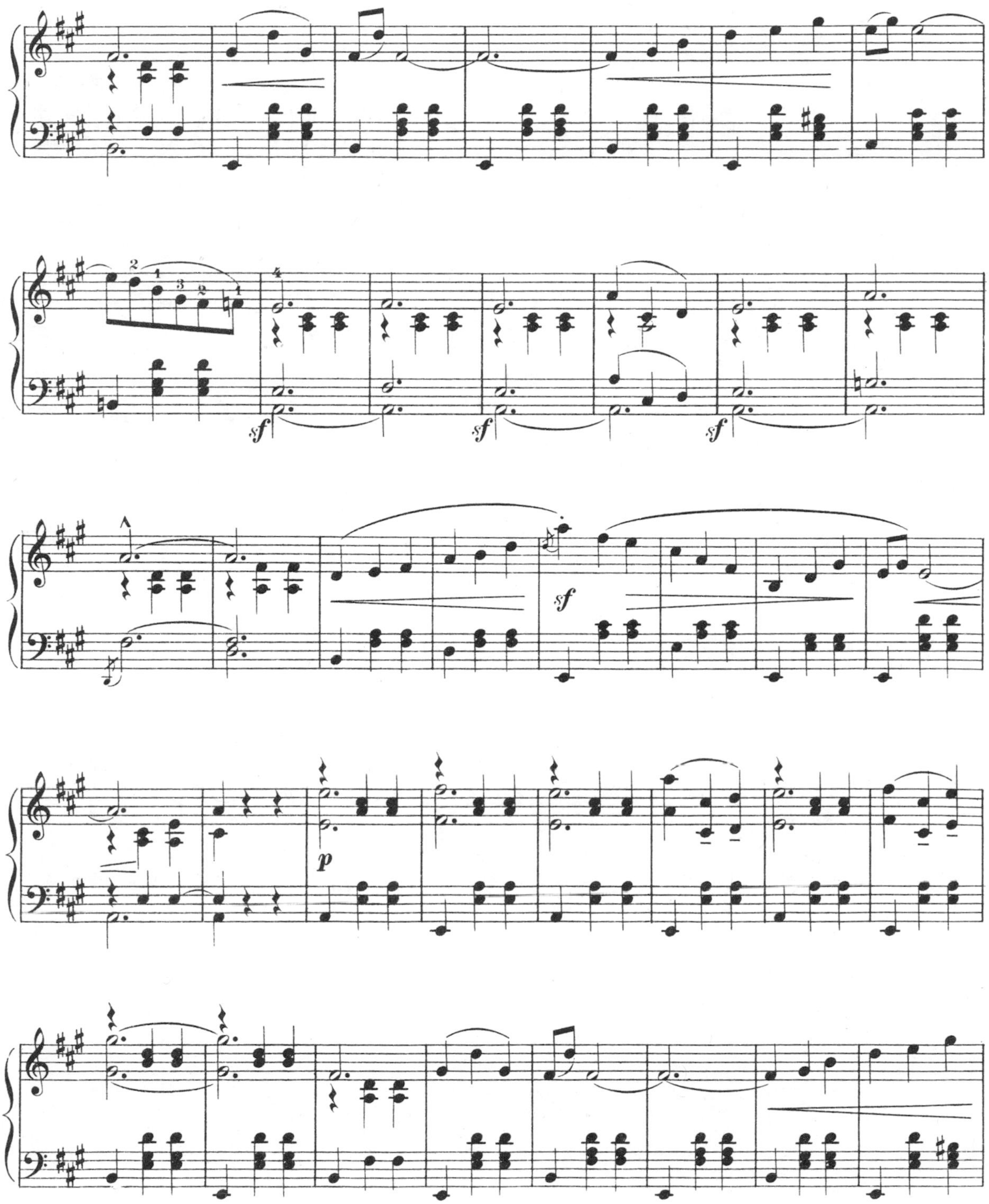

più f

sf

poco più a capriccio.

mf

string. e cresc. *dimin. e rall.* *a tempo*

animando

string. e cresc.

dimin. e rall.
a tempo

f con fuoco

meno
p e dimin.
rall. molto
lunga.

Più lento.
p

f
f
Più lento.
lento.
Presto.
legg.
pp
ppp

April Smile
Waltz

Maurice Depret. Op. 11

15283
31381

Printed in the U.S.A.

15283
81381

2.
Cantabile.
f
pp
1
2
leggiero
p
cresc.
dim.
f
pp
1
2

3.
p
f
1
pp
2
p
espress
p
f
1
pp

2
ff
p
poco cresc.
1
dim.
2
ff

Ballroom-Whispers

Ballgeflüster

Ped.
Ped.
mf
a tempo
riten poco
poco ritard.
p

Tempo I°
pp
simile
dim.
Ped.
Cantabile
p

mf armonioso
sfz
poco rall.
Ped.

Poco più mosso.
espressivo
mp
p
cresc.
poco rit.
p
pp
simile
Tempo I.
pp

dim.
sempre pianissimo
estinto sin'al Fine.
pp
pp
ppp

Dengozo

(Brazilian Maxixe-Tango)

Ernesto Nazareth
Arranged and edited by G. S. W.

1.
2.
senza ritard.
sfz
sfz

Con grazia
p
sfz
mf
p
sfz
p
1.
2.
p
mf

1.
2.
leggiero
p
f
1.
2.
p
mf
senza ritard.
sfz sfz

Y... ¿Como Le Vá?

Tango Argentino

On Motives by H. Herpin

J. Valverde

22882
31381

22882
31881

f
3
3
3
3
3

Exhibition March

Philipp Fahrbach, Jr. Op. 263

Trio.
f
p
mf
1
2

f Trombe
f
mf
f
1
2
mf
f
second time pp
cresc.
1
2
pp
Fine.

Standard-bearer March

Philipp Fahrbach, Jr. Op. 192

p
f
p
f
Fine.
Trio.
f
sf
p
f

March D.C.

Attack by the Uhlans

Revised and fingered by
Wm. Scharfenberg

Carl Bohm. Op. 213

ff con bravura.

poco rit.
a tempo.
p
ff
ff con bravura

ff
sempre ff
ff
fz
il Basso marc.
p dol.
cresc.
f
ffz
ffz
f

mf dol.
cresc. molto
brillante.
ff
ffz
pesante e rit.
a tempo.
p riten.
riten.
f
p

ff
Ped.
sempre ff
sfz

114
Friedrichs-Marsch
Josef Gungl. Op. 145
Aëroplane 2
Band 5
Battle 10
Birds 21
Calls 273
Chase 599
Chatter 28
Children 31
Chimes 259
Dances 39
Gavottes 39
Marches 102
Mazurkas 48
Minuets 54
Polkas 61
Tangos 94
Valses lentes 78
Valses 65
Doll 129
Festival 140
Fire-Fighting 151
Funeral 160
Grotesque 165
Gruesome 169
Happiness 202
Horror 173
Humorous 174
Hunting 186
Impatience 194
Joyfulness 202
Love-themes 209
Lullabies 231
Misterioso 242
Monotony 250
Music-box 254
National 261
Neutral 467
Orgies 487
Oriental 496
Parties 523
Passion 571
Pastorale 564
Pulsating 587
Purity 591
Quietude 591
Race 599
Railroad 608
Religioso 616
Sadness 621
Sea-Storm 651
Sinister 663
Wedding 671
Western 665

1.
2.
sfz
fp
Ped.
ff

Trio.
fp
f
p
ff
1.
2.
Marsch D.C.

With the Military

March

Philipp Fahrbach, Jr.

1
2
p
mf
1
2
mf

Trio.
f
p
f
March D.C.

Vienna March

Arranged by T. G. Shepard

J. Schrammel

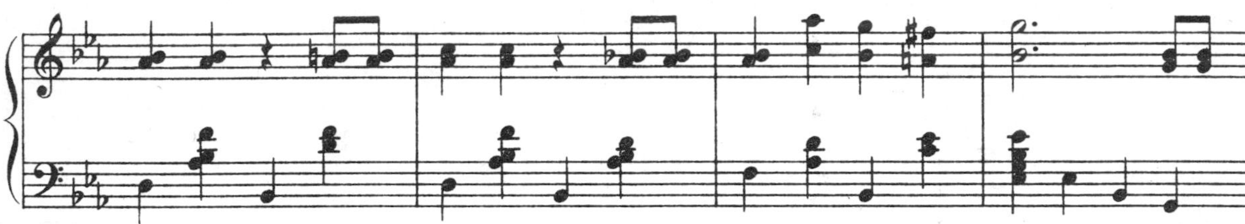

Trio.
p
p
ff

Finale.
ff
tr
p
f

Rheinland Regiment March

Johann N. Král

1.
2.
mf
Fine.
Trio.
p
f
p
f
cresc.
f
pp
1.
2.

f
p
f
f
p
sff
D. C. al Fine.

The Golden Wedding

Revised and fingered by
Wm. Scharfenberg

Gabriel-Marie

Andantino (𝅗𝅥 = 88)

mf
p
cresc.
f
p
sf
f
sotto voce
pp

20699
31381

decresc.
pp
cresc.
f
rit.
p
Ped.
Ped.
a tempo
sf
tr
p

mf
cresc.
allargando

Poupée Valsante

Edited and fingered by
Louis Oesterle

Ed. Poldini

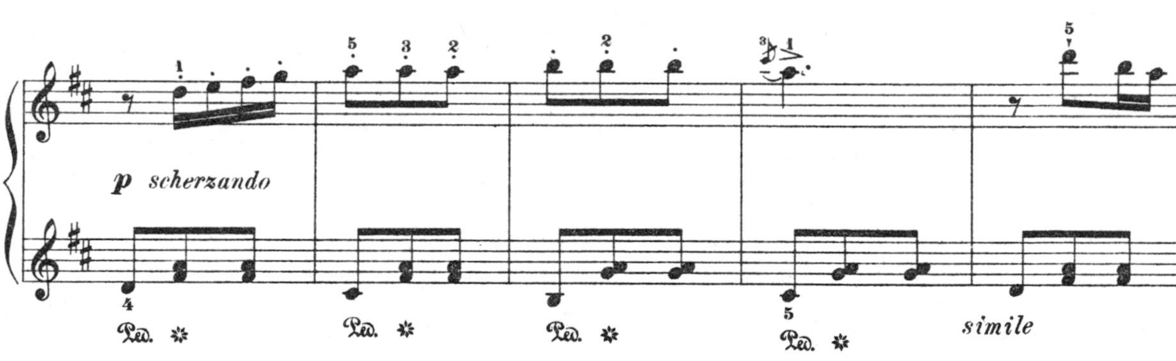

16965 r

pp

p
pp
p
1.
2.

p
cantabile
Ped.
dimin.
p
f

dimin.
p
pp
ppp
smorzando
Ped.

Aëroplane 2
Band 5
Battle 10
Birds 21
Calls 273
Chase 599
Chatter 28
Children 31
Chimes 259
Dances 39
Gavottes 39
Marches 102
Mazurkas 48
Minuets 54
Polkas 61
Tangos 94
Valses lentes 78
Valses 65
Doll 129
Festival 140
Fire-Fighting 151
Funeral 160
Grotesque 165
Gruesome 169
Happiness 202
Horror 173
Humorous 174
Hunting 186
Impatience 194
Joyfulness 202
Love-themes 209
Lullabies 231
Misterioso 242
Monotony 250
Music-box 254
National 261
Neutral 467
Orgies 487
Oriental 496
Parties 523
Passion 571
Pastorale 564
Pulsating 587
Purity 591
Quietude 591
Race 599
Railroad 608
Religioso 616
Sadness 621
Sea-Storm 651
Sinister 663
Wedding 671
Western 665
140
Marche Héroïque
Franz Schubert
Moderato
f
fp
fp
fp
fp
p
cresc.
p
cresc.
f
sf

ff
pp
p
cresc.
sf
sf
fp
fp
fp
fp
8

Aëroplane 2
Band 5
Battle 10
Birds 21
Calls 273
Chase 599
Chatter 28
Children 31
Chimes 259
Dances 39
Gavottes 39
Marches 102
Mazurkas 48
Minuets 54
Polkas 61
Tangos 94
Valses lentes 78
Valses 65
Doll 129
Festival 140
Fire-Fighting 151
Funeral 160
Grotesque 165
Gruesome 169
Happiness 202
Horror 173
Humorous 174
Hunting 186
Impatience 194
Joyfulness 202
Love-themes 209
Lullabies 231
Misterioso 242
Monotony 250
Music-box 254
National 261
Neutral 467
Orgies 487
Oriental 496
Parties 523
Passion 571
Pastorale 564
Pulsating 587
Purity 591
Quietude 591
Race 599
Railroad 608
Religioso 616
Sadness 621
Sea-Storm 651
Sinister 663
Wedding 671
Western 665
142
cresc.
cresc.
Fine.
Trio.
15645

p
pp
dolce
cresc
pp
p
D. C. al Fine.

Coronation March
Giacomo Meyerbeer
Molto maestoso
ff
ff
ff
p

ff

ff
p
cresc.

15645
31381

March and Procession of Bacchus

From the Ballet "Sylvia"

L. Delibes

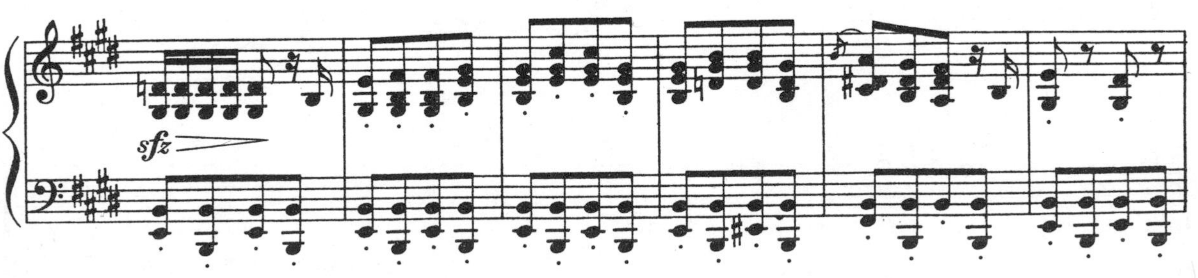

sfz
sfz
sfz
sfz
sfz
sfz

cresc.

Hurry No. 2

(For scenes of great excitment, duels, fights, *etc.*)

Otto Langey

D. C.

Agitato No. 2

(Heated argument, or intense situation, leading to a fight or riot, *etc.*)

J. E. Andino

Tempo I°
cresc.
sempre cresc.
ff
mf
ff
Molto vivace
ff strepitoso
ffz
fz
fz

Furioso No. 3

(Depicting Riots, Tumultuous Scenes, *etc.*)

Otto Langey

f *ff*

1. 2. *Fine*

mf *f*

mf

f *mf* *cresc. poco a*

poco *f*

D. C. al Fine

Card Trio

From the opera "Carmen," Act III

G. Bizet

8
sf
pp
8
poco sf
p

From the Ballet-Suite "Salammbò"

H. Arends

Moderato maestoso

ff

8

8

f

f

ff

8

8

f dim.

D. C.

Marche funèbre

From the Sonata Op. 35

F. Chopin

Printed in the U. S. A

Andante Pathétique No. 1

(Prison scene, intense or dramatic situations, deep emotion)

R. Schumann
Arranged by Otto Langey

espressivo
p
pp
più f
f
dim.
p
1.
2.
D.S.

Funeral March

F. Mendelssohn. Op. 62, No. 3

a) It has become popularly known as a "Funeral March" because it was played –as orchestrated by Moscheles– at Mendelssohn's funeral.

25496
31381

a) These two figures may be played by both hands

Misterioso No. 1

(For depicting gruesome scenes, stealth, *etc.*)

Otto Langey

poco a poco cresc.
f
3
1.
2.
p
3
p
mf
cresc.
f
p
1.
2.
D. S

Tanz aus Jölster

(Dance from Jölster)

Edvard Grieg. Op. 17, No. 5

staccato
pp
Più mosso.
molto cresc.
Coda.
non legato
sostenuto
ff più allegro e sempre string.

Misterioso Infernale

For uncanny situations

Gaston Borch

cresc.
rall.
cresc.

Misterioso No. 2

(For dark scenes, burglaries, shadowing, tracking a fugitive or victim, *etc.*)

Adolf Minot

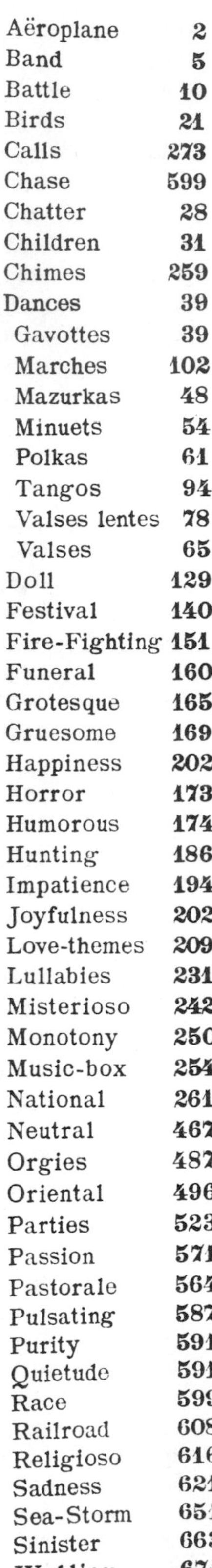

D. C.

Overture to "Phèdre"

Andante molto sostenuto

J. Massenet

Abduction of the Bride

from the Second Peer Gynt Suite

Allegro furioso

Edvard Grieg. Op. 55

Humoresque

P. Tschaikowsky. Op. 10, No. 2

Printed in the U. S. A.

Semplice, ma espress.
cresc.

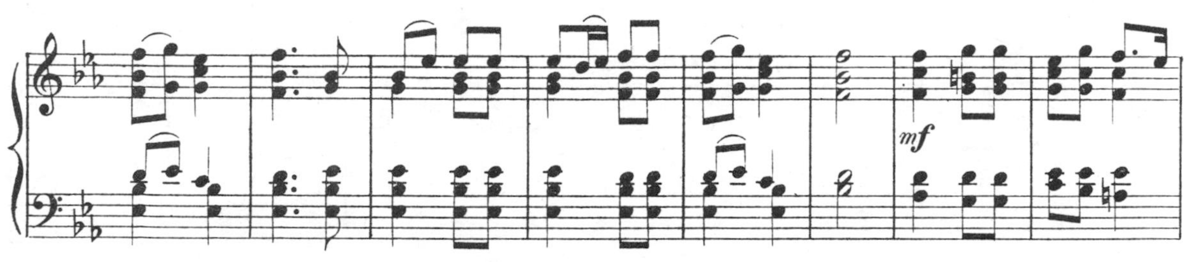
mf

dim.
p
pp

poco cresc. rit.
sf

p

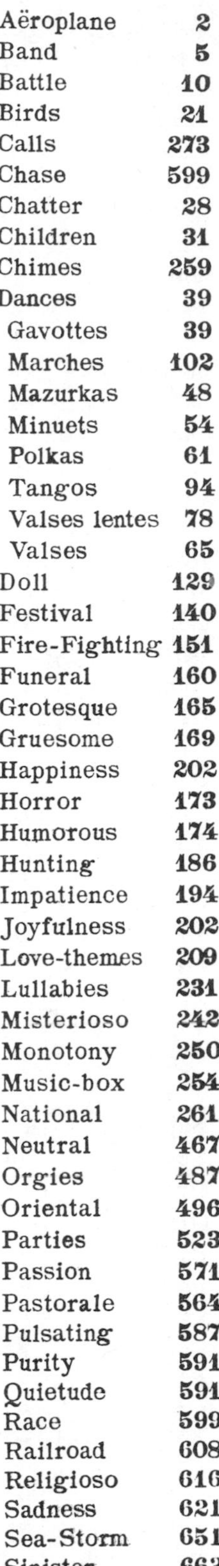

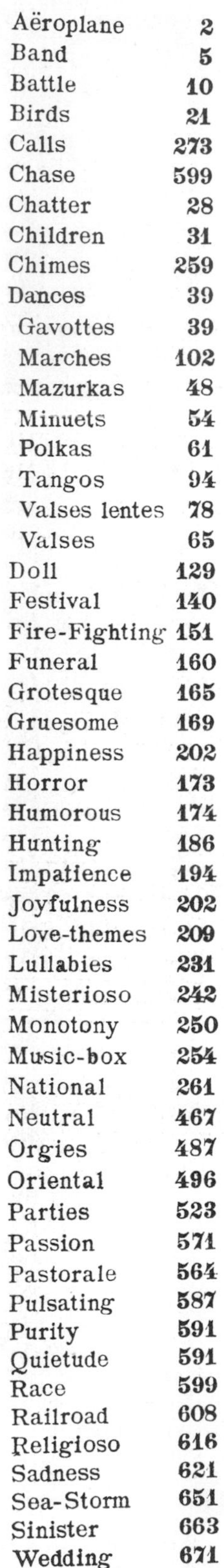

pp

rit.
poco cresc.
mf
a

tempo
rit.
poco più
f
mf
a tempo

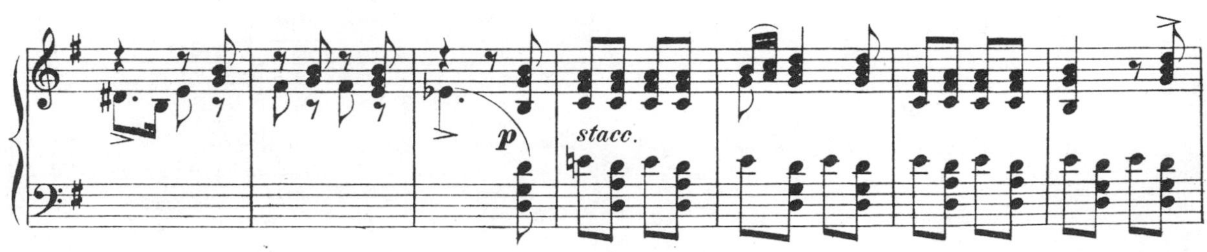

p
stacc.

cresc.
ff
stacc.
p
cresc.
sempre stacc.
poco
a poco dim.

Curious Story
Kuriose Geschichte

Revised and fingered by Wm. Scharfenberg

Stephen Heller

Printed in the U.S.A.

f
p
molto ri - te - nu - to.
espress.
a tempo.
m.s.
sfz
cresc.
Vivo.
ritard.

15542
31381

Printed in the U. S. A.

Stabbe-Laaten

(Humoristic Dance)

Edvard Grieg. Op. 17, No. 18

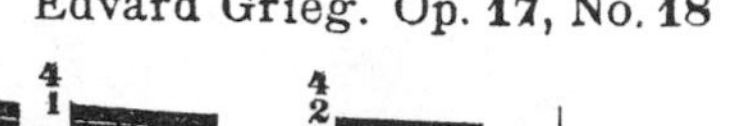

Allegro.

p cresc. f pp p f p fz sopra

Coda.
sostenuto

Le Coucou

Edited and fingered by
Louis Oesterle

A. Arensky. Op. 34, No. 2

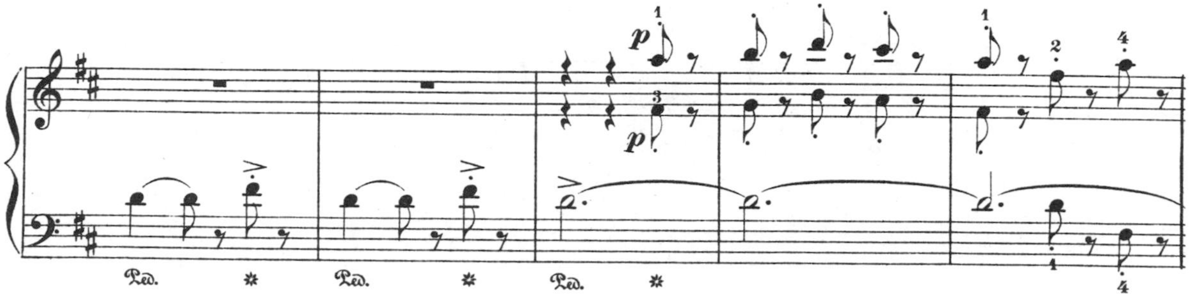

23697

cresc.

cresc.
(2da ritenuto)
1.
2.
Fine.

Jagdlied

Hunting Song

Edited and fingered by
Max Vogrich

Rasch, kräftig
Allegro con spirito (♩. = 120)

R. Schumann. Op. 82

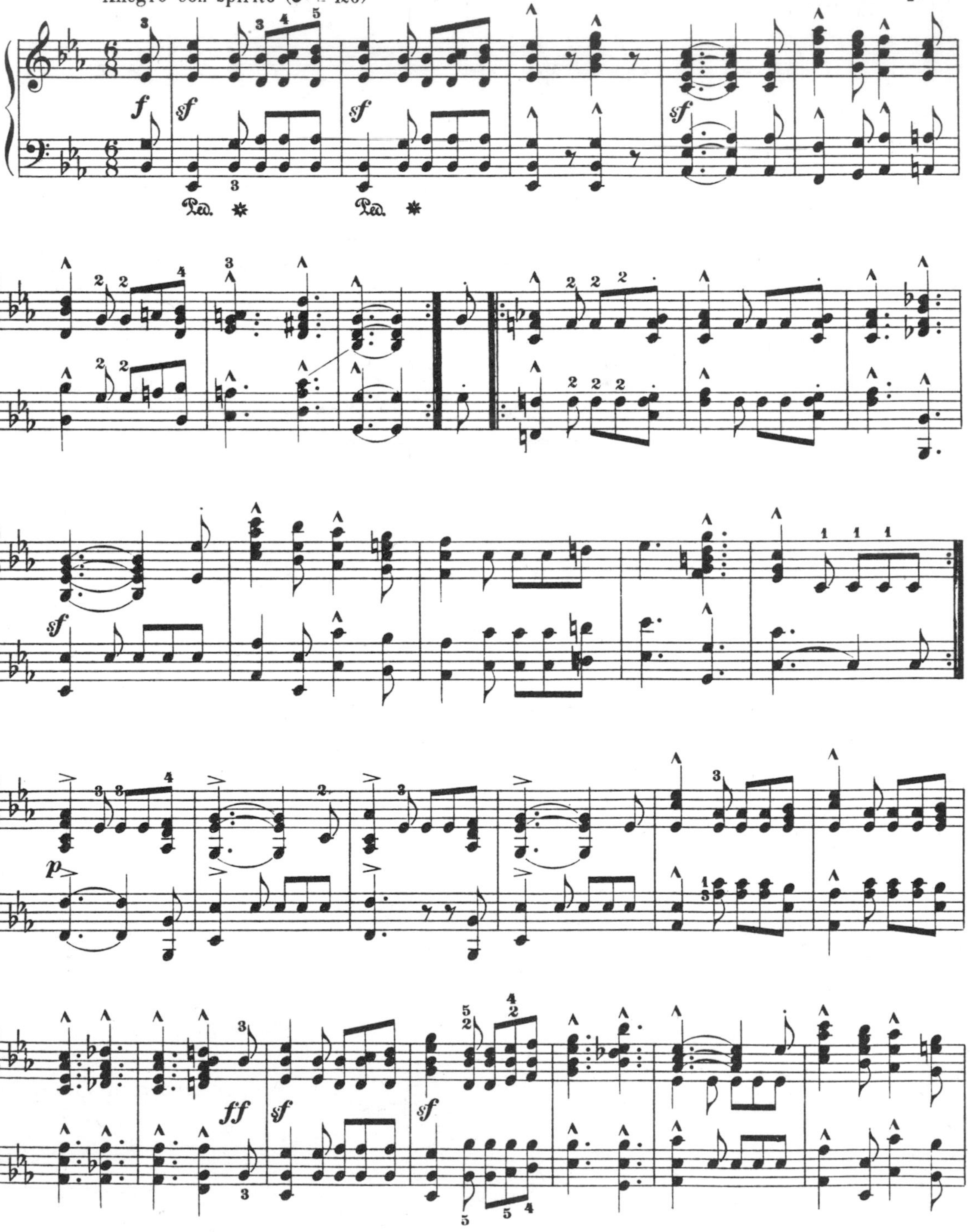

17827 r

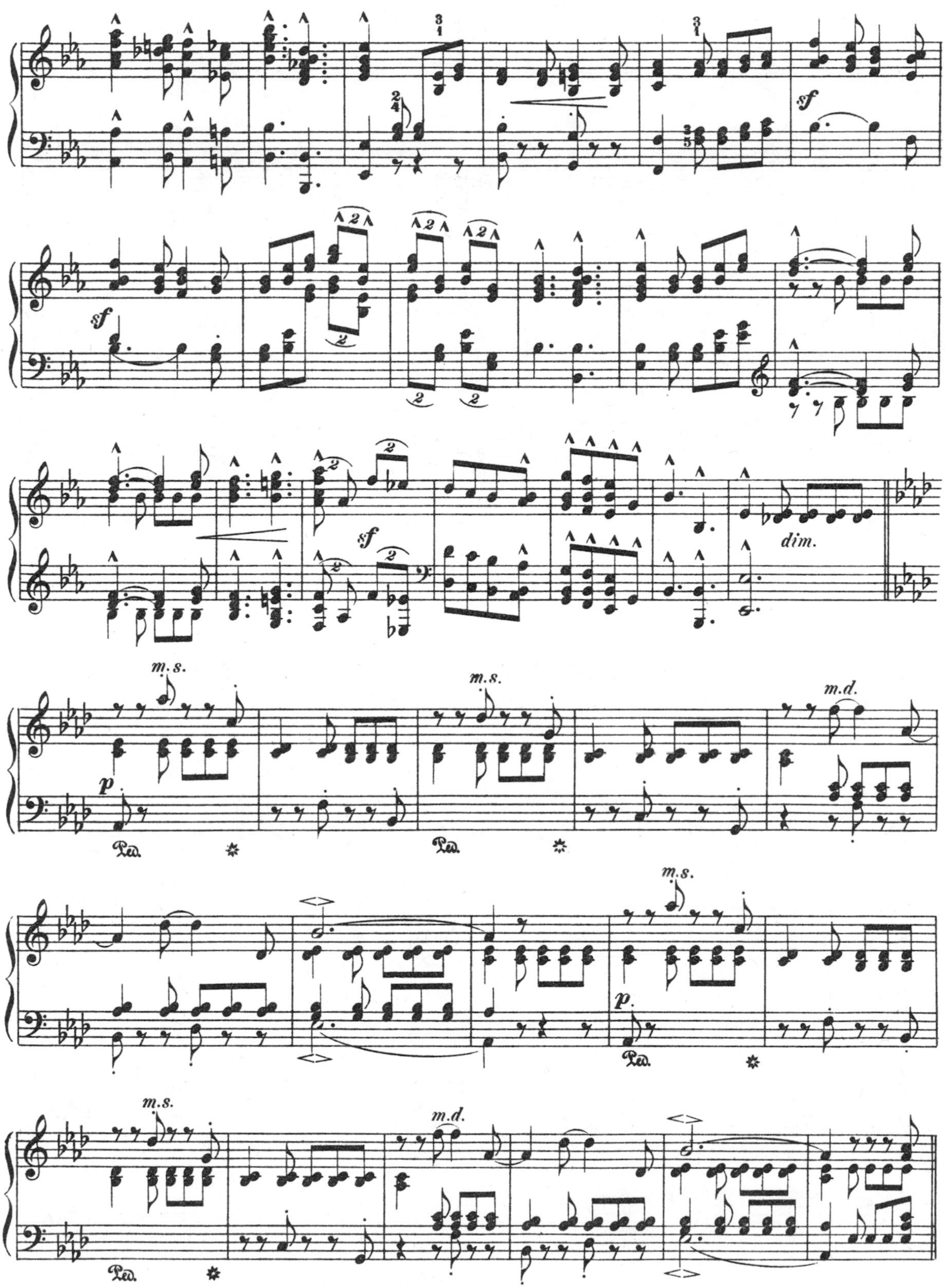

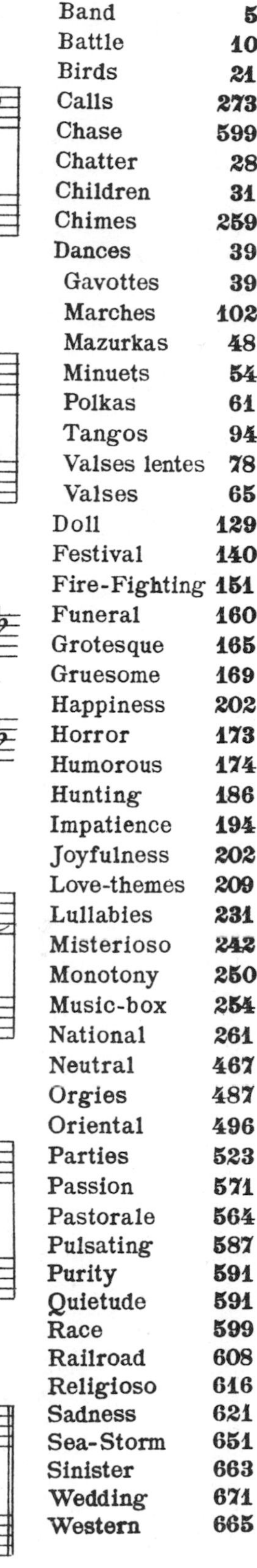

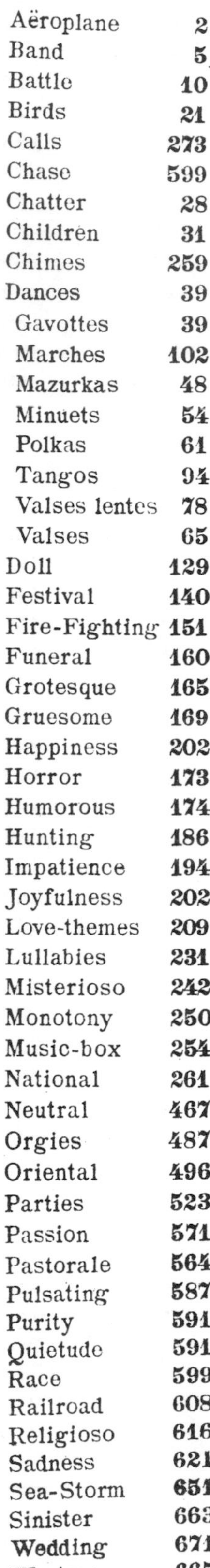

Jagd-Fanfare
Hunter's Call

H. Reinhold. Op. 39

Jägerliedchen
Hunting Song

*) Frisch und fröhlich.
Vivace, gajo. (♩. = 112)

R. Schumann

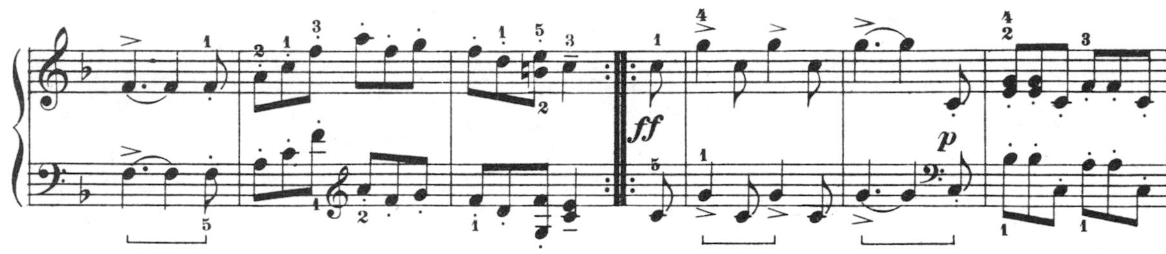

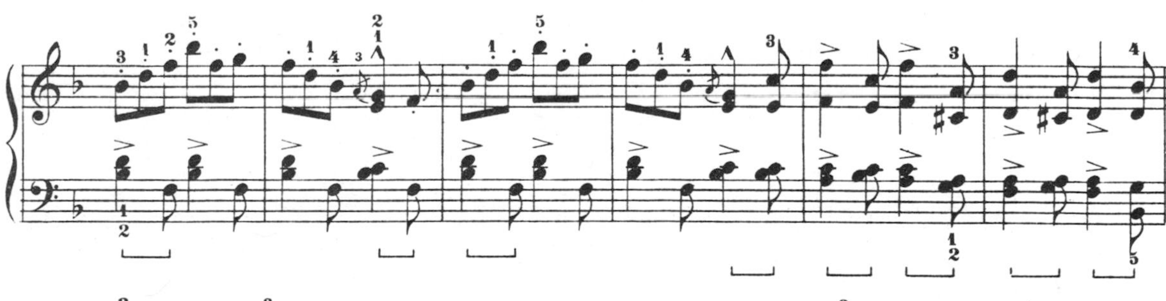

*) Die mit dem Staccato-punkt bezeichneten Noten werden mit losem Handgelenk ausgeführt. Dasselbe Verfahren im nächst folgendem Stücke.

*) Notes marked with the staccato dot, are to be played with a loose wrist. The same holds good for the piece that follows.

13036c

Printed in the U. S. A.

The Hunter's Horn

Revised and fingered by
Wm Scharfenberg

A. Schmoll. Op. **50**

ff
p
cresc.
mf
cresc.
Moderato.
ff
p
Allegro.
p
mf
f
ff
mf

Impatience
Song without Words

Revised and fingered by
Wm Scharfenberg

Louis Gregh

10290 r

a tempo.
f allarg.
cresc.
f
p
molto rit.
a tempo.
mf
ten.
poco rit.
p
a tempo.
molto rit.
mf

appassionato.
f
a tempo.
dim. rit.
mf
ten.
poco rit.
dim.
p molto rit.
pp

Untiring Search

Revised and fingered by
Wm. Scharfenberg

H. Stiehl. Op. 64, No. 4

f
fz
f
dim.
mf
cresc.
f
fz
p
mf
dim.
p
rit.

Song without Words
Homeless

F. Mendelssohn. Op. 102, No. 1

a) Special attention should be given to the strict maintainance of this very original rhythm.

cresc.
cresc.

p
cresc.
f
dimin.
p
dimin.
sempre Pedale

Happy Wanderer

Revised and fingered by
Wm Scharfenberg

A. Jensen

decresc.
1.
2.
Fine.

p
1.
2.
cre - - scen - -
do.
f

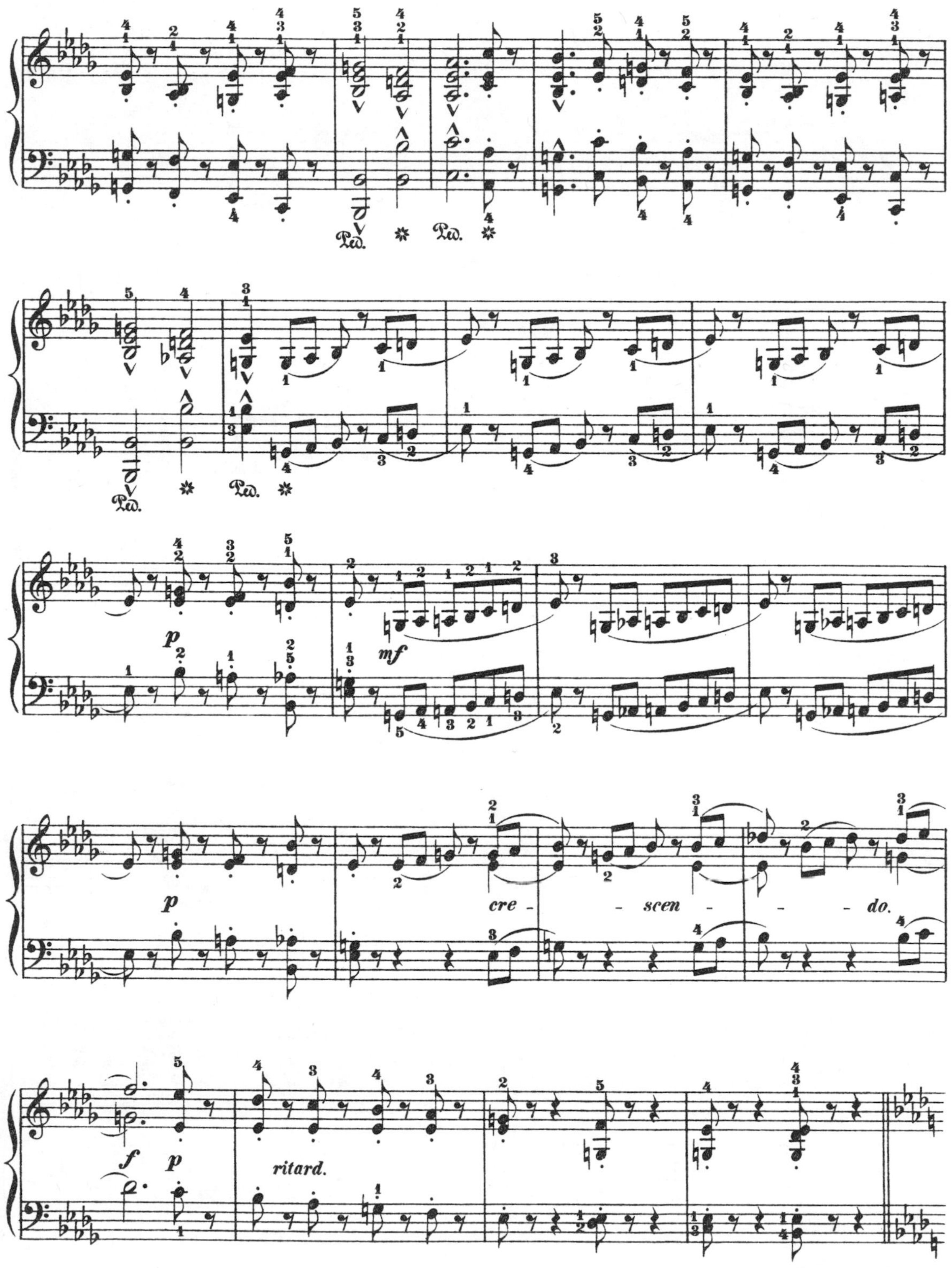

cre - scen - do.

ritard.

D. C. al Fine.

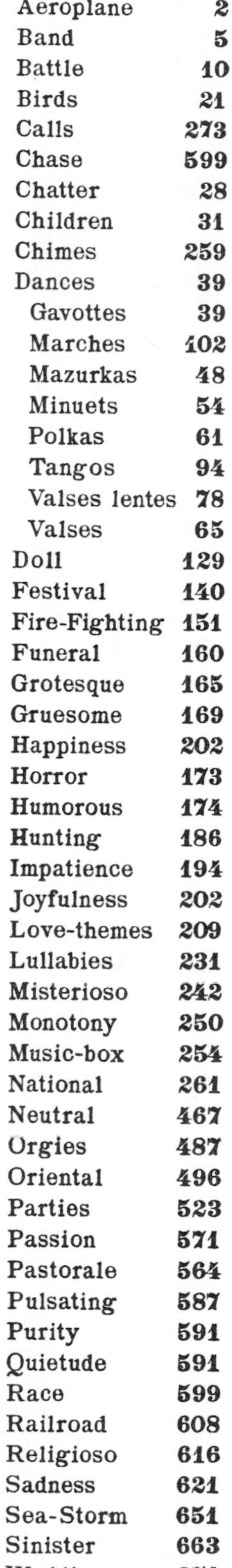

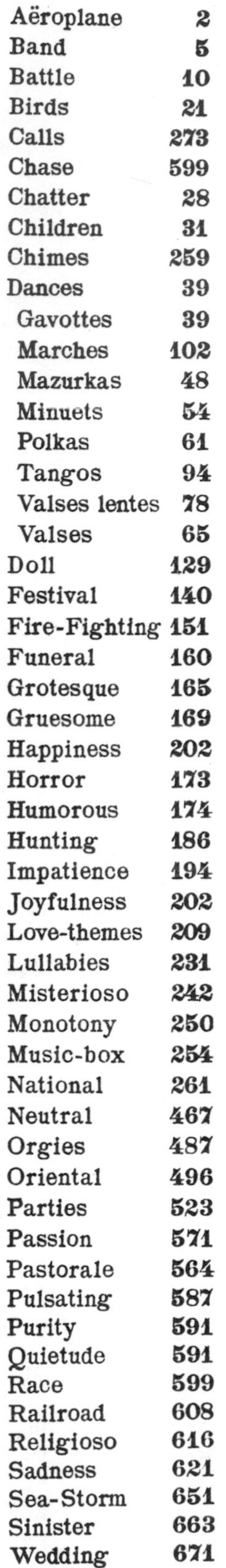

À la Polka

Zdenko Fibich. Op. 41, No. 10

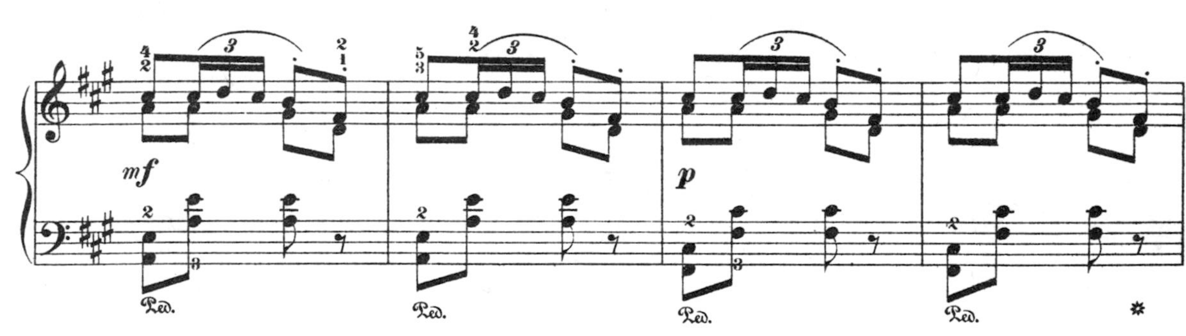

l.h. r.h.
rit.
a tempo
Fine

cantabile
mf
sopra
p
pp
mf
rit.
Da Capo al Fine.

The Old Mother

Anton Dvořák
Transcribed by Erno Rapée

con duolo
mf
p
pp
cresc.
affettuoso
rit.
a tempo
dim.
morendo
pp

Romance

25432 C
31381

mf
f
p
f
ff
p

mf
cresc.
f
ff
p
cresc.
ff
dim.
p

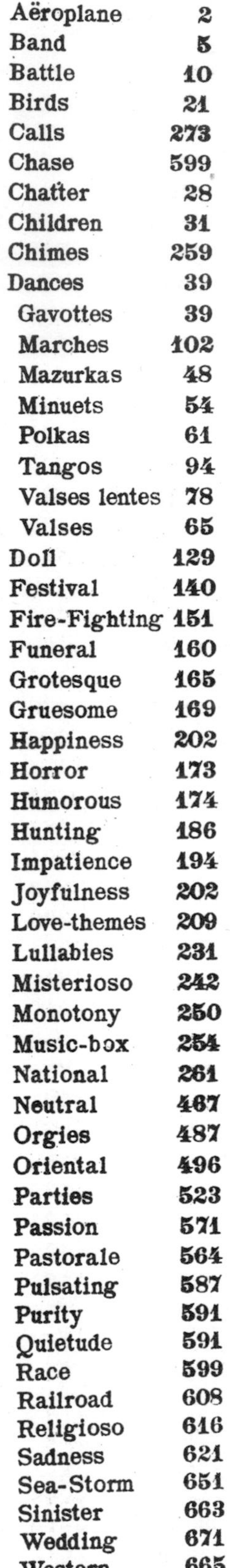

p

mf
rit.

pp una corda

rall.
lento
ppp

Valse

J. Brahms

p
p
poco cresc.
dolce

Poem

Zdenko Fibich
Transcribed by Erno Rapée

pp subito
cresc. molto
f
ff
mf
p
marcata la melodia
8
pp
ppp

Cavatina

Revised and fingered by
Wm Scharfenberg

Joachim Raff
Transcribed by E. Pauer

7530

smorzando.
cresc.
cresc.

marcato
p
pp
f
p
f
grandioso.
rinf.
Ped.

stringendo
a tempo
smorz.

Love - Song

Rudolf Friml. Op. 85bis, No. 3

Moderato appassionato

accel.
animato
p
mf
p
mf
marcato
molto rit.

a tempo
cresc.
accel.
cresc.
f
ff
rit.
Ped.

Melody

Edited and fingered by
W. K. Bassford

A. Rubinstein. Op. 3, No. 1

12598

cresc.
string.
p
rit.
Tempo I.
p
cresc.

string.
rit.
Tempo I.
p
cresc.
p
p
R.H.
pp

Chant d'Amour
Love-Song

Edited and fingered by
Louis Oesterle

I. J. Paderewski. Op. 10, Nº 2

con
molto cresc.
ff
passione
pesante
ff
string.
pesante
mf poco rall.
pp
pp ben marcata la melodia
string: molto
ritard.
p
più lento
p
l.h.
ppp

Berceuse

Lullaby

Revised and fingered Edition

A. Iljinsky. Op. 13

Poco andante

Ped. Ped.

23697

poco rall.
dim.
a tempo.
p
Ped.
una corda.
Ped.
dim. e rit.
pp

Lullaby

N. Louise Wright. Op. 30

Andante con moto

dim.
p
pp
dim. e rit.
pp
morendo
ppp
Ped.

Berceuse
Edited and fingered by
Max Vogrich
Allegretto tranquillo. (♩ = 92.)
Edvard Grieg. Op. 38, No. 1
p
rit.
a tempo.
una corda.
ppp
morendo.
15542

Con moto.
p tre corde.
rit.
a tempo.
p
Ped.
ritard.
Ped.
più p
una corda
Ped.
a tempo.
pp tre corde.
Ped.
Ped.
cresc. e
strello.
Ped.
Ped.
Ped.
Ped.

15542

f
dim. e ritard. molto.
a tempo.
p
pp
morendo.
ppp
15542

Sérénade

Edited and fingered by
Louis Oesterle.

Marian Sokołowski. Op. 4, Nº 3.

l.h.
Un poco più mosso.
p dolce e cantabile
cresc.
Ped.

un poco agitato
allargando
calando
rall.
Tempo I.
l.h.
rit.
p
r.h.
a tempo
marcato il canto

l. h.
cresc.
r. h.
f
ff
rall.
sotto voce
più p una corda
decresc. e perdendosi sin' al Fine.
Ped. sempre
ritard. poco a poco
ppp

Zug der Zwerge

March of the Dwarfs

Edited and fingered by
Louis Oesterle

Edvard Grieg. Op. 54, No. 3

14835
31381

Allegro Misterioso Notturno

For stealthy action in the dark

Gaston Borch

28301
31381

p
mf
f
cresc.
più f
dim.
1.
2.
pp

Agitato Misterioso

Fear, anxiety, suspense, ominous situations, *etc.*

Otto Langey

1.
2.
Fine
mf
pp
cresc.
1.
2.
D.S. al Fine

The Erlking

Le Roi des Aulnes

Revised and fingered by
Wm. Scharfenberg

Franz Schubert
Transcribed by Stephen Heller

il canto marcato.

Prelude

(No. 15)

F. Chopin

ff
fz dimin.
p
cresc.
f
p
dim. e rit.
Ped.

Bådnlåt

Cradle-song

Edvard Grieg. Op. 66, No. 15

poco rit.
f
ffz
p
Tempo I.
p
cantabile
p
ritardando
legato
pp

Music-Box

Rudolf Friml. Op. 69

21802 c

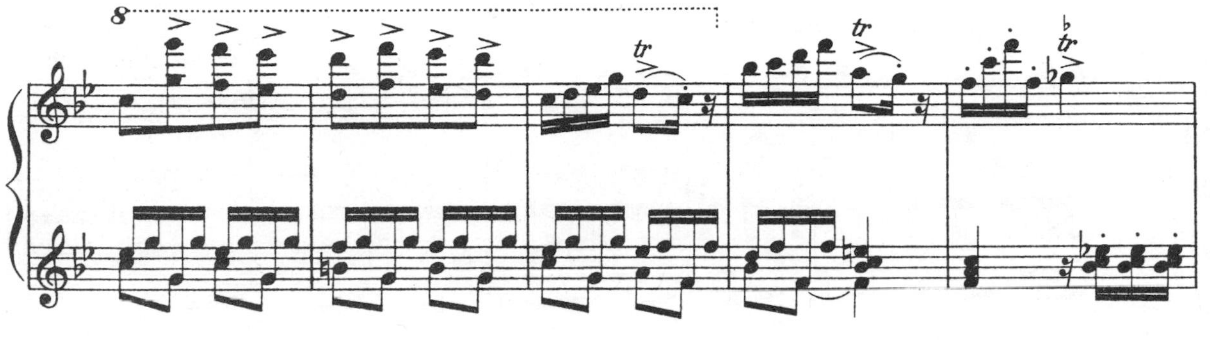
8
tr
tr
tr

tr
cresc.
tr

tr
rit.
8
a tempo

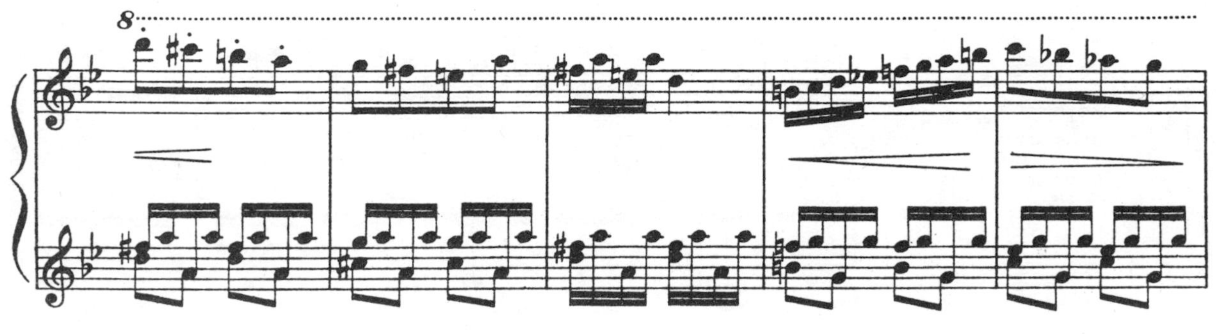
8

rit.
a tempo
molto ritenuto
pp

Une Tabatière à Musique

Valse-Badinage

Edited and fingered by
Louis Oesterle

Anatole Liadow. Op. 32

D. C.

Klokkeklang
Ringing Bells

Edited and fingered by
Louis Oesterle

Edvard Grieg. Op. 54, No. 6

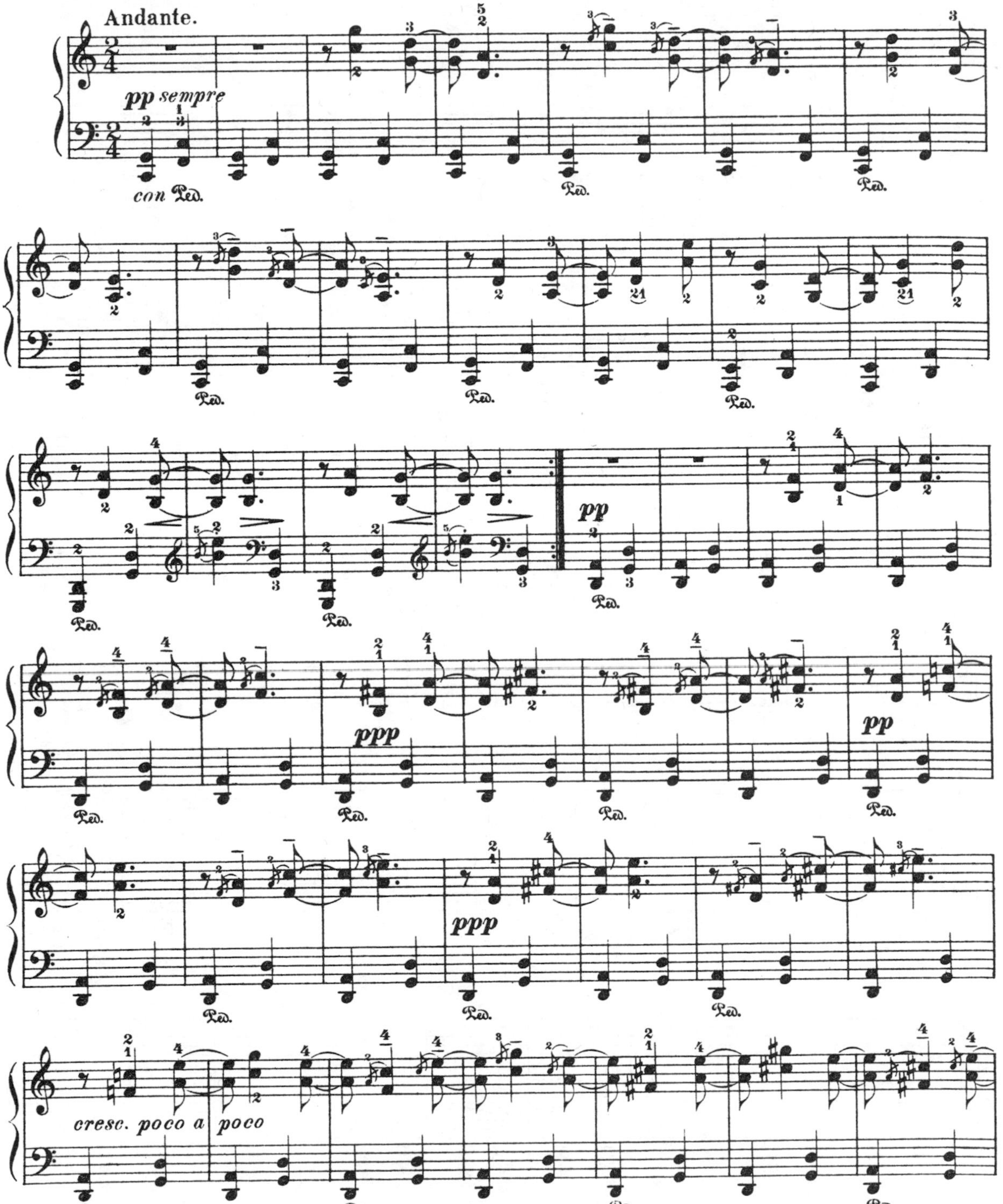

Andante.

pp sempre

con Ped.

pp

ppp

pp

ppp

cresc. poco a poco

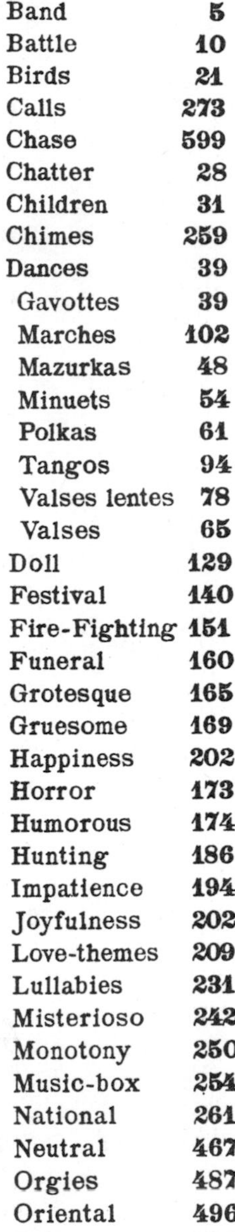

15542
31381

sempre più cresc.
molto
fff
dimin. molto e poco ritard.
Tempo I.
pp
dimin.
pp
molto
ff
p
pp
morendo

United States of America

The Star-Spangled Banner

National Hymn

John Stafford Smith

America ("My country, 'tis of thee")

Patriotic Air

This Melody also serves as a National Hymn in the following countries:

England
Denmark
Sweden
Norway
Switzerland
***
Prussia
Bavaria
Saxony
Wurtemberg
Weimar
Mecklenburg
Hamburg

Henry Carey

Maestoso

Hail Columbia

Patriotic Air

Maestoso

ff

p

3
3
ff
p
ff
3
3

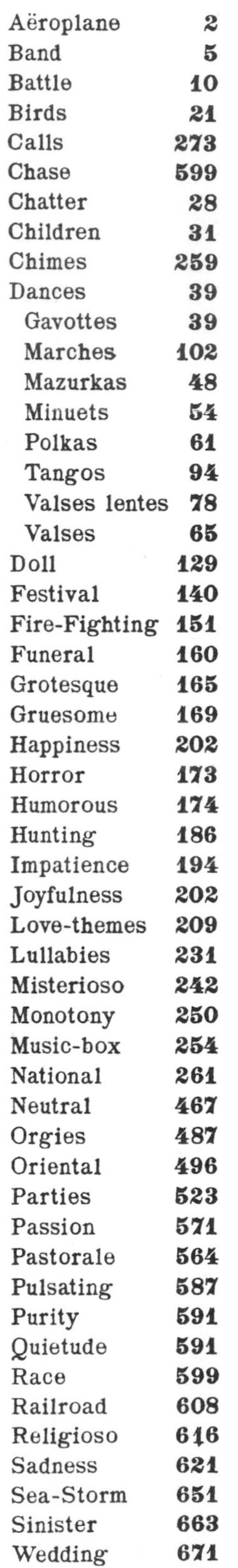

The Red, White and Blue

"Columbia, the Gem of the Ocean"

Marziale

ff

fz

Fine

ff

24342

The Battle-Cry of Freedom

George F. Root

Moderate marching time

f

1. Yes, we'll ral - ly round the flag, boys, we'll ral - ly once a - gain,
2. We are spring - ing to the call of our broth - ers gone be - fore,
3. We will wel - come to our num - bers the loy - al, true and brave,
4. So we're spring - ing to the call from the East and from the West,

ff

Shout - ing the bat - tle - cry of Free - dom, We will ral - ly from the hill - side, we'll
Shout - ing the bat - tle - cry of Free - dom, And we'll fill the va - cant ranks with a
Shout - ing the bat - tle - cry of Free - dom, And al - tho' they may be poor not a
Shout - ing the bat - tle - cry of Free - dom, And we'll hurl the reb - el crew from the

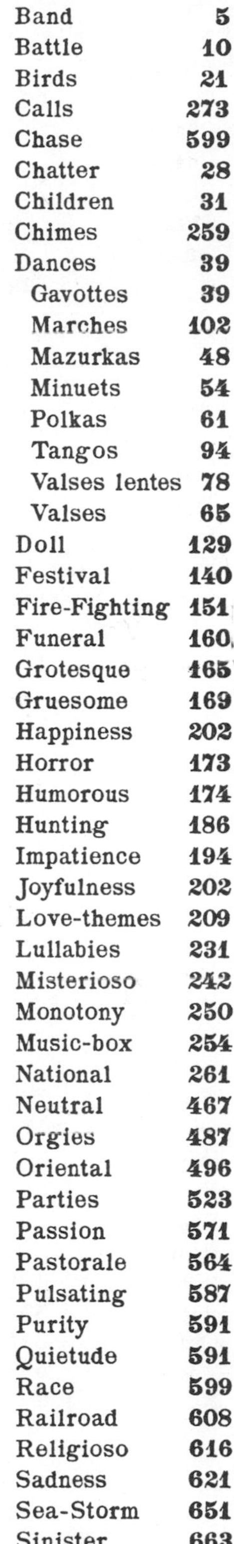

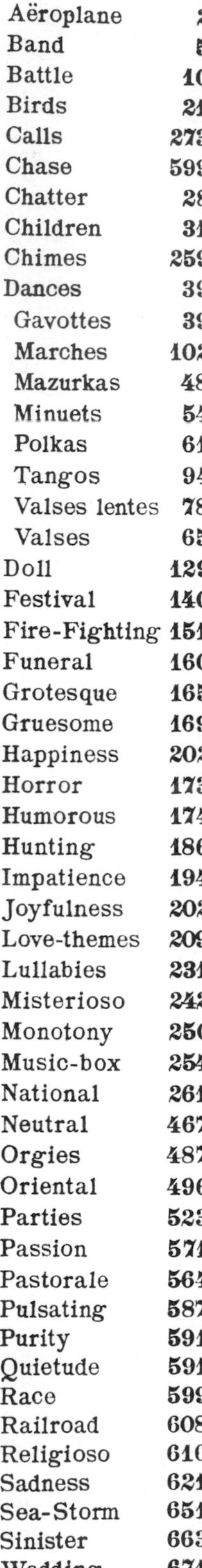

gath - er from the plain, Shout - ing the bat - tle - cry of Free - dom!
mil - lion free - men more, Shout - ing the bat - tle - cry of Free - dom!
man shall be a slave, Shout - ing the bat - tle - cry of Free - dom!
land we love the best, Shout - ing the bat - tle - cry of Free - dom!

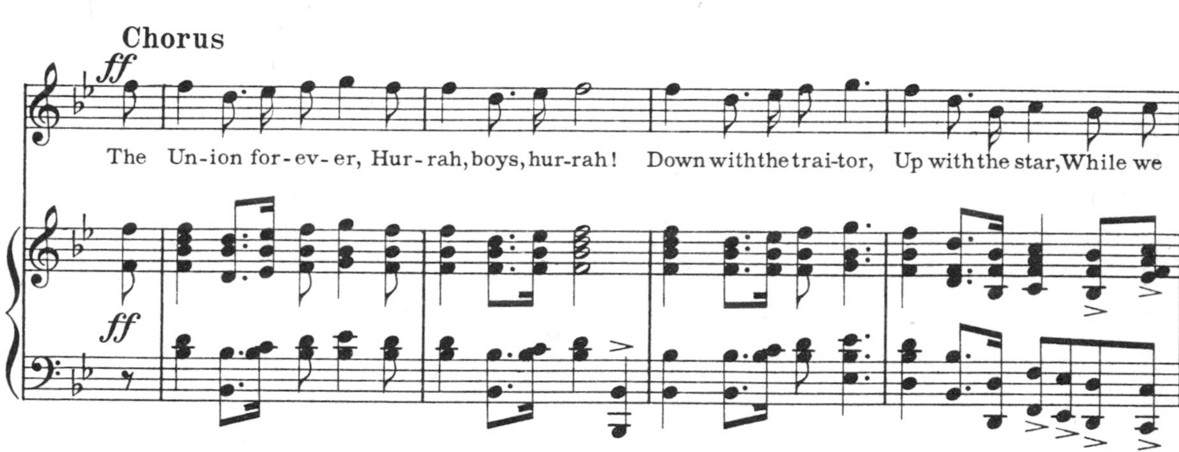

Chorus
ff
The Un-ion for-ev-er, Hur-rah, boys, hur-rah! Down with the trai-tor, Up with the star, While we
ff

ff
ral - ly round the flag, boys, ral - ly once a-gain, Shout-ing the bat-tle-cry of Free - dom!
ff

Battle Hymn of the Republic

Julia Ward Howe

Composer unknown

loos'd the fate-ful light'ning of His ter-ri-ble swift sword; His truth is march-ing on.
read His righteous sen-tence in the dim and flar-ing lamps; His day is march-ing on.
he-ro born of wo-man crush the ser-pent with his heel, Since God is march-ing on.
swift, my soul, to an-swer Him, be ju-bi-lant, my feet! Our God is march-ing on.
die to make men ho-ly, let us die to make men free, While God is march-ing on.
Chorus
f
Glo-ry! Glo-ry Hal-le-lu-jah, Glo-ry! Glo-ry Hal-le-lu-jah!
f
cresc.
ff
Glo-ry! Glo-ry Hal-le-lu-jah! His truth is march-ing on.
cresc.

269
Tramp! Tramp! Tramp!
Words and melody by
George F. Root
Brisk Marching time
mf
mf
1. In the pris - on cell I sit, Think - ing, moth - er dear, of you, And our
2. In the bat - tle front we stood, When their fierc - est charge they made, And they
3. So with - in the pris - on cell We are wait - ing for the day That shall
mf
bright and hap-py home so far a - way, And the tears they fill my eyes, Spite of
swept us off, a hun-dred men or more, But be - fore we reached their lines They were
come to o-pen wide the i - ron door, And the hol - low eye grows bright, And the
Aëroplane 2
Band 5
Battle 10
Birds 21
Calls 273
Chase 599
Chatter 28
Children 31
Chimes 259
Dances 39
Gavottes 39
Marches 102
Mazurkas 48
Minuets 54
Polkas 61
Tangos 94
Valses lentes 78
Valses 65
Doll 129
Festival 140
Fire-Fighting 151
Funeral 160
Grotesque 165
Gruesome 169
Happiness 202
Horror 173
Humorous 174
Hunting 186
Impatience 194
Joyfulness 202
Love-themes 209
Lullabies 231
Misterioso 242
Monotony 250
Music-box 254
National 261
Neutral 467
Orgies 487
Oriental 496
Parties 523
Passion 571
Pastorale 564
Pulsating 587
Purity 591
Quietude 591
Race 599
Railroad 608
Religioso 616
Sadness 621
Sea-Storm 651
Sinister 663
Wedding 671
Western 665

all that I can do, Tho' I try to cheer my com-rades and be gay.
beat-en back dis-mayed, And we heard the cry of vic-t'ry o'er and o'er.
poor heart al-most gay, As we think of see-ing home and friends once more.
Chorus
Tramp, tramp, tramp, the boys are march-ing, Cheer up, com-rades, they will
come! And be-neath the star-ry flag we shall
breathe the air a-gain Of the free land in our own be-lov-ed home.

Yankee Doodle

Author unknown

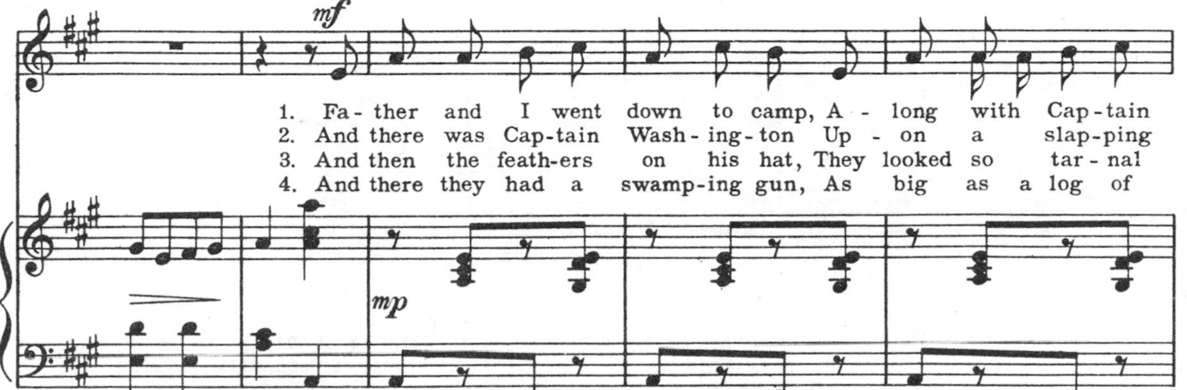

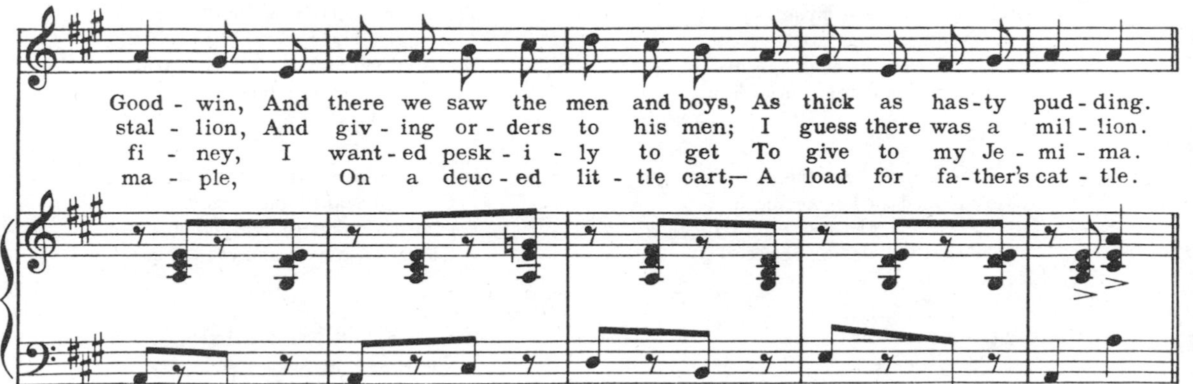

Aëroplane 2
Band 5
Battle 10
Birds 21
Calls 273
Chase 599
Chatter 28
Children 31
Chimes 259
Dances 39
Gavottes 39
Marches 102
Mazurkas 48
Minuets 54
Polkas 61
Tangos 94
Valses lentes 78
Valses 65
Doll 129
Festival 140
Fire-Fighting 151
Funeral 160
Grotesque 165
Gruesome 169
Happiness 202
Horror 173
Humorous 174
Hunting 186
Impatience 194
Joyfulness 202
Love-themes 209
Lullabies 231
Misterioso 242
Monotony 250
Music-box 254
National 261
Neutral 467
Orgies 487
Oriental 496
Parties 523
Passion 571
Pastorale 564
Pulsating 587
Purity 591
Quietude 591
Race 599
Railroad 608
Religioso 616
Sadness 621
Sea-Storm 651
Sinister 663
Wedding 671
Western 665

5.
And every time they fired it off
It took a horn of powder;
It made a noise like father's gun,
Only a nation louder.

6.
I went as near to it myself
As Jacob's underpinin';
And father went as near again—
I thought the deuce was in him.

7.
(It scared me so, I ran the streets,
Nor stopped as I remember,
Till I got home, and safely locked
In granny's little chamber.)

8.
And there I see a little keg;
Its heads were made of leather,
They knocked upon't with little sticks,
To call the men together:

9.
And there they'd fife away like fun,
And play on corn-stalk fiddles;
And some had ribbons red as blood,
All bound around their middles.

10.
The troopers too, would gallop up,
And fire right in our faces;
It scared me almost half to death,
To see them run such races.

11.
Uncle Sam came there to change
Some pancakes and some onions
For 'lasses cakes to carry home
To give his wife and young ones.

12.
But I can't tell you half I see,
They kep up such a smother;
So I took my hat off, made a bow,
And scampered home to mother.

Six Bugle-Call Pieces

Reveille

Arthur Tomlinson

In quick time

Taps

Adjutant's Call

28024
21381

The General's March

Assembly March

Moderato

mf

f

p

mf

f

To the Colors

In quick time

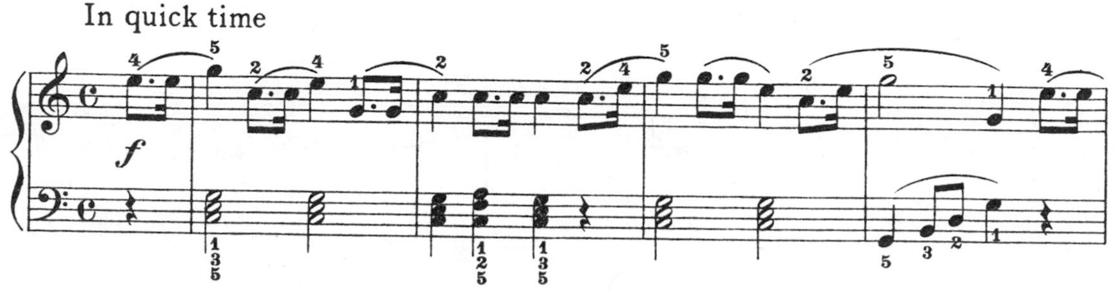

mf *f* *mf* *p* *f* *p* *f*

Southwestern Idyl

(Country life, love-scenes, also Mexican)

Irénée Berge

f
mf
3
p
3
D.S. al Coda
CODA
mf
dim.
p

Dixie Land
Southern Air

Patriotisches Lied

Dan Emmet

My Old Kentucky Home

Folk-Song

Stephen Collins Foster

Old Folks at Home

"Swanee River"

Folk-Song

Stephen Collins Foster

Plantation Melody

Recorded by Alice Haskell

Harmonized by Arthur Farwell

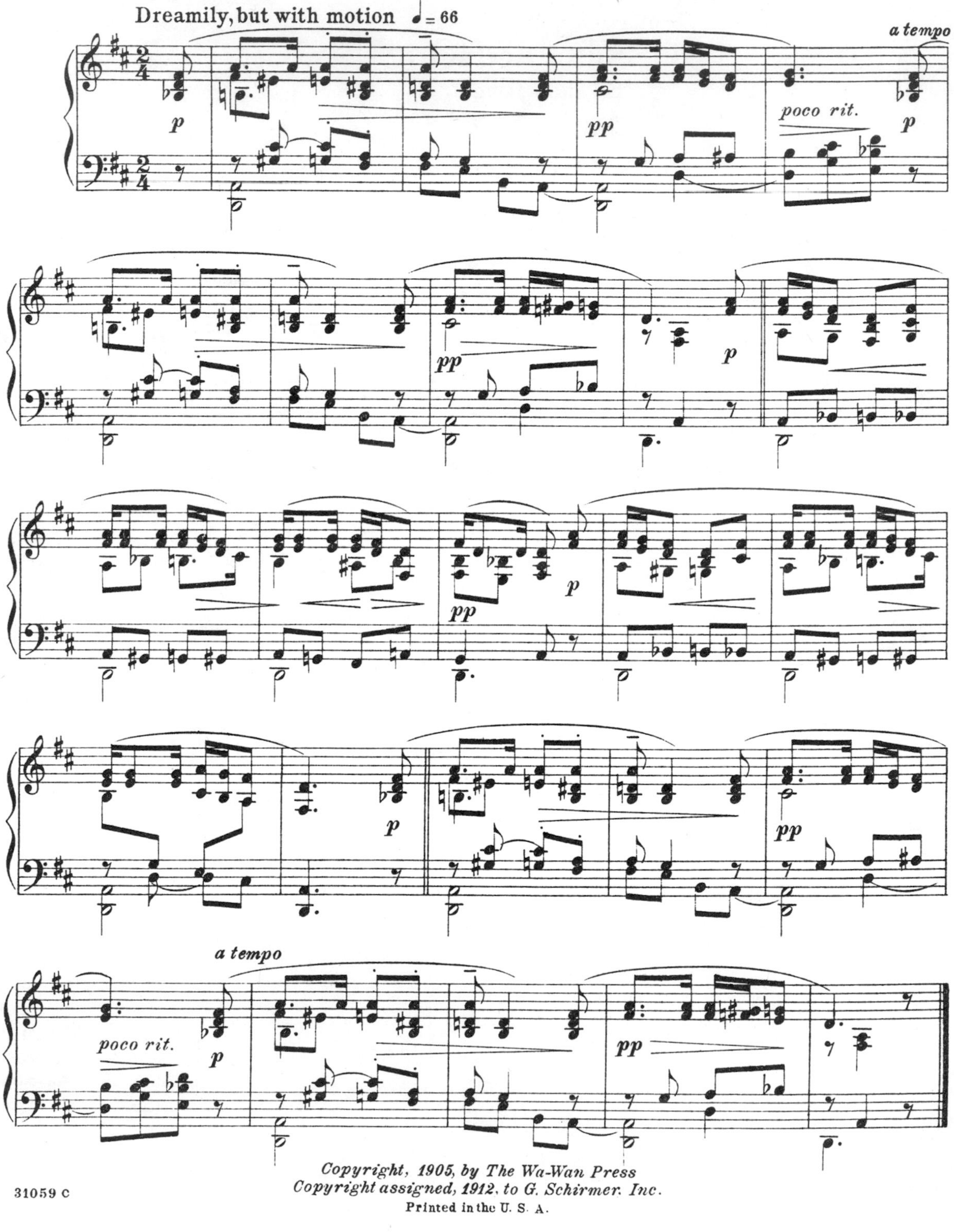

Dreamily, but with motion ♩= 66

p *pp* *poco rit.* *a tempo* *p*

pp *p*

pp *p*

p *pp*

poco rit. *p* *a tempo* *pp*

College Songs March

Th. G. Shepard

Printed in the U. S. A.

f
mf
f
mf
f

287

Alma Mater

Fair Harvard

Andante moderato

Gaudeamus

Moderato

Upidee

Moderato

We Won't Go Home till Morning

Allegro moderato

Aëroplane 2
Band 5
Battle 10
Birds 21
Calls 273
Chase 599
Chatter 28
Children 31
Chimes 259
Dances 39
Gavottes 39
Marches 102
Mazurkas 48
Minuets 54
Polkas 61
Tangos 94
Valses lentes 78
Valses 65
Doll 129
Festival 140
Fire-Fighting 151
Funeral 160
Grotesque 165
Gruesome 169
Happiness 202
Horror 173
Humorous 174
Hunting 186
Impatience 194
Joyfulness 202
Love-themes 209
Lullabies 231
Misterioso 242
Monotony 250
Music-box 254
National 261
Neutral 467
Orgies 487
Oriental 496
Parties 523
Passion 571
Pastorale 564
Pulsating 587
Purity 591
Quietude 591
Race 599
Railroad 608
Religioso 616
Sadness 621
Sea-Storm 651
Sinister 663
Wedding 671
Western 665
292
Nancy Lee
Arranged by
S. Jackson
With spirit
Stephen Adams
1. Of all the wives as e'er you know, Yeo - ho! lads,
2. The har - bour's past, the breez - es blow; Yeo - ho! lads,
3. The boa - s'n pipes the watch be - low, Yeo - ho! lads,
ho! Yeo - ho! yeo - ho! There's none like Nan - cy Lee, I trow,
ho! Yeo - ho! yeo - ho! 'Tis long ere we come back, I know,
ho! Yeo - ho! yeo - ho! Then here's a health a - fore we go,
25000
31381
Printed in the U. S. A.

— Yeo - ho! — lads, ho! — yeo - ho! See, there she stands an'
— Yeo - ho! — lads, ho! — yeo - ho! But true an' bright from
— Yeo - ho! — lads, ho! — yeo - ho! A long, long life to
f
p
waves her hands, up - on — the quay, An' ev - 'ry day when I'm a - way She'll
morn till night my home — will be, An' all so neat, an' snug an' sweet, For
my sweet wife, and mates — at sea; An' keep our bones from Da - vy Jones, wher-
watch — for — me, An' whis - per low, when tem - pests blow, for Jack, — at
Jack — at — sea, An' Nan - cy's face to bless the place, an' wel - come
e'er — we — be, An' may you meet a mate as sweet as Nan - cy
rall.
a tempo
sea. Yeo - ho! — lads, ho! — yeo - ho! The sai - lor's
me. Yeo - ho! — lads, ho! — yeo - ho! The sai - lor's
Lee. Yeo - ho! — lads, ho! — yeo - ho! The sai - lor's
rall.
p a tempo

wife the sai-lor's star___ shall be! Yeo - ho!___ we_ go a -
wife the sai-lor's star___ shall be! Yeo - ho!___ we_ go a -
wife the sai-lor's star___ shall be! Yeo - ho!___ we_ go a -
cross___ the_ sea,___ The sai - lor's wife the sai - lor's
cross___ the_ sea,___ The sai - lor's wife the sai - lor's
cross___ the_ sea,___ The sai - lor's wife the sai - lor's
f
star___ shall be, The sai - lor's wife his star shall
star___ shall be, The sai - lor's wife his star shall
star___ shall be, The sai - lor's wife his
1.&2.
colla voce
be.___
be.___
3.
star shall be.___
colla voce
ff

"Rocked in the Cradle of the Deep"

Edited by Max Spicker

J. P. Knight

mf
espress.
save. I know thou wilt not slight my call, For
thou dost mark the spar-row's fall! And calm and peaceful is my
p
sleep, Rock'd in the cra-dle of the deep; And
pp
calm and peaceful is my sleep, Rock'd in the cradle of the deep.

p
And
mf
dolce
such the trust that still were mine, — Tho' stormy winds — swept o'er the brine, Or
ff
tho' the tem-pest's fie-ry breath — Rous'd me from sleep — to wreck and
ff
death! In o - cean cave still safe with Thee, The
p
espress.
p

calando
germ of immortal-i - ty; And calm and peaceful is my sleep,
pp
Rock'd in the cradle of the deep; And calm and peaceful is my
pp
poco allarg.
cra - dle of the deep.
sleep, Rock'd in the cra-dle of the deep.
allarg. col canto
5
a tempo
mf
p allarg. al fine

Jingle Bells

Allegro moderato

Hark! The Herald Angels Sing

F. Mendelssohn

Adeste Fideles

John Reading

Holy Night

Sally in Our Alley

Home, Sweet Home

H. R. Bishop

Love's Old, Sweet Song

J. L. Molloy

Robin Adair

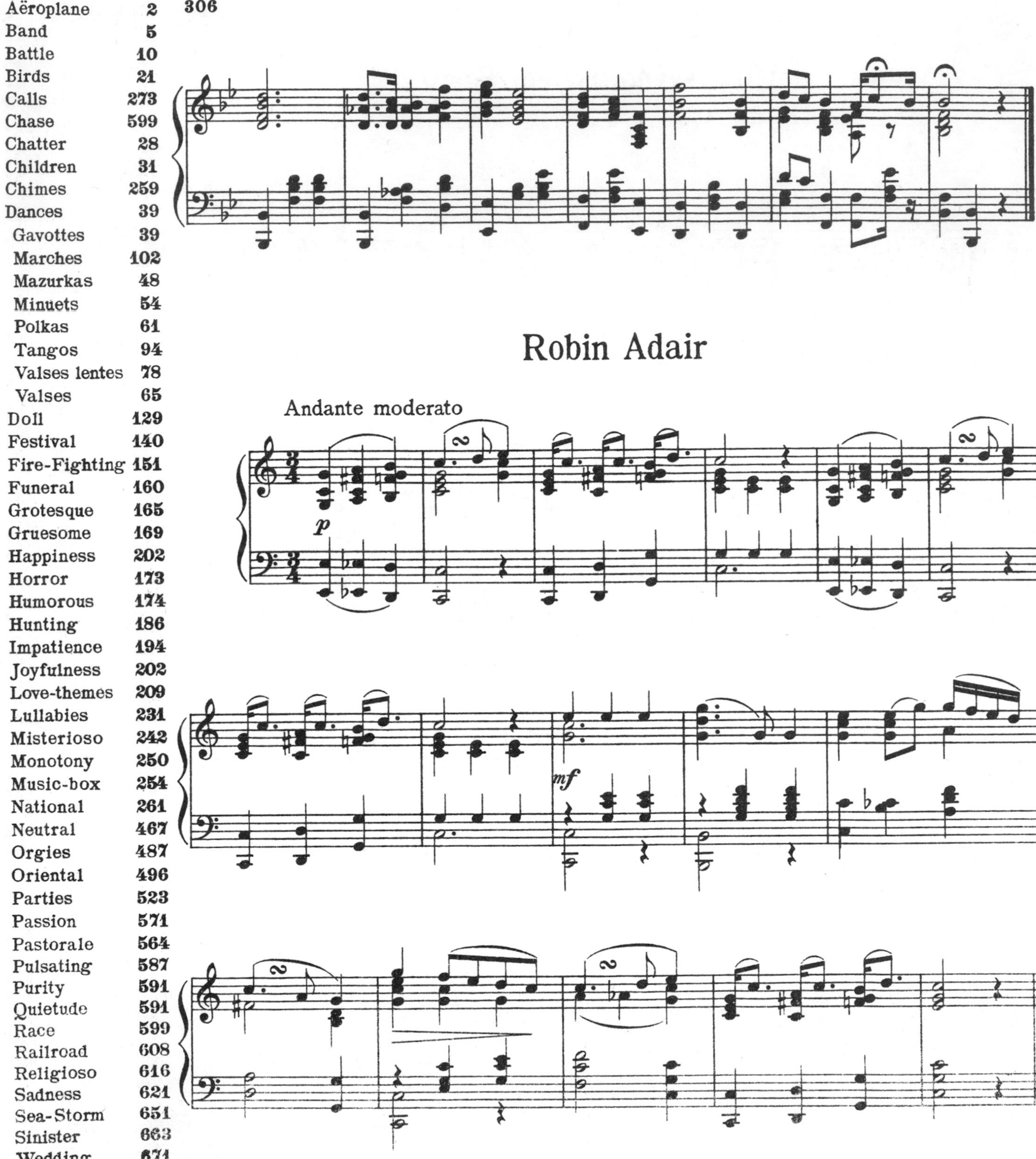

Alice, Where Art Thou

J. Ascher

poco animato
mf
rit.
a tempo
cresc.
f
p
8

Listen to the Mocking-Bird

Alice Hawthorne

When You and I Were Young, Maggie

J. A. Butterfield

Argentine Republic

National Hymn

f
p
mf
p
sfz
24342

fz
Allegro
mf
Lento
p
Allegro
rall.
f

Australian Patriotic Air

"O, du mein Österreich"

Patriotic Air

Moderato

p dolce

Cornet Solo

(or Clar. or Viol. or Fl.)

p

mf

tr

pp

f

rit.

a tempo

mf

Bohemia

Patriotic Air

24342

Belgium
National Hymn

Brazil

National Hymn

Bulgaria

(National Hymn

The Maple-Leaf for Ever

Canadian Patriotic Song

Vive la Canadienne

Patriotic Song

24342

Chili

National Song

24342
31381

China

National Hymn

United States of Colombia

National Hymn

Fine
D.C. al Fine

Costa Rica

National Song

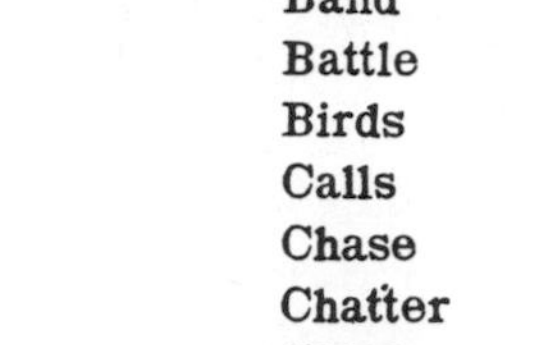

Cuba

National Song

Edited and fingered by
Max Vogrich

Danzas

Ignazio Cervantes

14384 c

Con passione.
2.
p
espress.
f con fuoco
Poco più vivo
mf
f
p
f
dolce
marcato
f
p
p a capriccio
14384

Japan

National Hymn

China

National Hymn

Chinese-Japanese

Otto Langey

tr
tr
tr
rit.
a tempo
cresc.
f
mf
mf
mf
mf
dim.
dim.
p
dim.
rit.
pp

Suite of Three Oriental Sketches

No. 2. In a Chinese Tea-Room

Otto Langey Op. 158, No. 2

p languido
Più mosso
mf
Tempo I°
a tempo
dim.
poco riten.
pp

pp
p
cresc.
f pesante
a tempo
p
cresc.
f
dim.
p
Allegro (♩=136)
mf
f

f
espress.
dim.
rall.
Tempo I°
sfz
mp
p
pp
p

pp
p
cresc.
f pesante
p dolce
poco accel.
mf
poco rall.
a tempo
p
poco rall.
a tempo
l.h.
rall.
p
pp

Chinese Lullaby

From "East Is West"
As sung by Ming Toy

Words and Music by
Robert Hood Bowers

NOTE: Song (a) is in Ming Toy's "Pigeon English"; Song (b) in the good English she learns later in the play.– It is first sung in pure Chinese.

b)
Moderato
mp
poco rubato
A rip - ple I seem On life's mys - tic
(Harp)
p
ben sostenuto
stream, Tossed at the wa - ters' will; So I
dare dream I'll be, Like the poor rip - ple, free; When the
slow
rit.
(Harp)
trou - bled wa - ters grow still. A still.
1.
2.
dim.
pp

Fuji-Ko

A Japanese Intermezzo

Harry Rowe Shelley

28808 C
31881

1

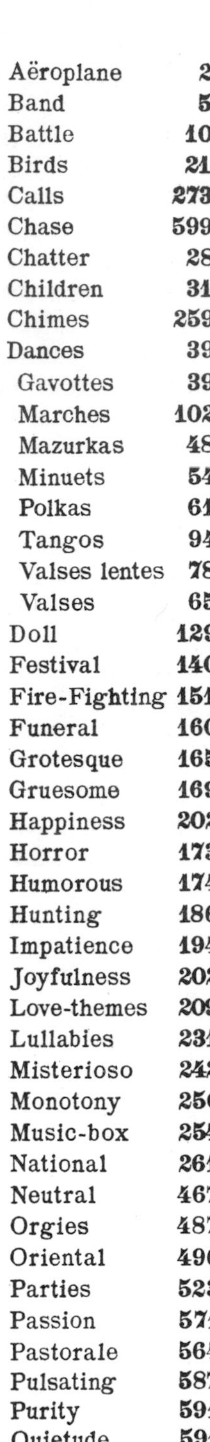

Cantabile

1

2
p

f

D.C. al 𝄋

CODA
pp

Denmark

Patriotic Air

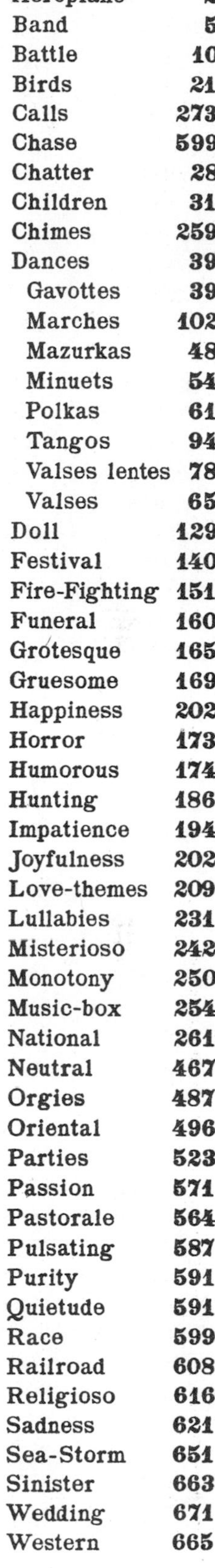

England

God Save the King

Henry Carey

Maestoso

Rule Britannia

Patriotic Air

Maestoso

ff

mp

f

"Drink to me only with thine eyes"

Ben Jonson (1573 - 1637)

Old English Air
Date uncertain

Printed in the U. S. A.

thirst_ that from the soul_ doth rise, Doth ask a drink di - vine,
pp
cresc.
But might I of Jove's nec - tar sip, I would not change for
thine!
mf
cresc.
I sent thee late a ros - y wreath, Not so_much hon'-ring thee
pp

As giv - ing it a hope that there_ It could not with - er'd
be; ______ But thou_ there - on didst on - ly breathe And
sent'st it back to me; ______ Since when it grows, and
pp
cresc.
smells, I swear, Not of_ it - self, but thee!
mf

France

La Marseillaise

National Hymn

Partant pour la Syrie
Patriotic Air

Chant du départ

Patriotic Air

Mourir pour la Patrie

Patriotic Air

Germany

Die Wacht am Rhein

National Hymn

Stimmt an mit hellem, hohen Klang

National Song

Greece
National Hymn
Marcia
f
D.C.
Hawaii
National Hymn
Moderato
f
p
f
p
f
p
f
31381

Oloha, oe

National Song

Mijn Neêrlandsch Bloed

National Hymn

Dios Salve a Honduras

National Song

Hungary

National Song

Rákóczy March

Patriotic Air

24342

f
p
f
p
1.
2.
3
p
Fine
f
p
p 3
D.S. al Fine

Slavic Dance

Edited and fingered by
Clarence Adler

Anton Dvořák. Op. 72

dim.
mf
dim.
p
dim.
pp
ritard.
stacc.
mf
a tempo
p
mf
pp
p
ritard.

a tempo
mf
Ped.
p
dim.
pp
ritard.
a tempo
p legato
fz
f
p
fz
p

molto espressivo
fz
p
fz
p
pp
fz
dim.
p
Ped.
Ped.
pp
Ped.
ritard.
a tempo
f
ffz
ffz
ff
dim.

mp
espressivo
p
dim.
pp
ritard.
a tempo
mp
mf
f
p
pp
pp
fz
mf
f
pp

Indian Agitato

Dramatic excitement for Indian emotional scenes, rivalry, jealousy, expectancy, apprehension, *etc.*

Otto Langey

Poco meno mosso
Fine
D.C. al Fine

Indian War-Dance

Irénée Bergé

f
f
f
ff
cresc.
fff
D.S. al
CODA
f
ff

Indian War-Dance

Gaston Borch

28313
31381

f
ff
poco dim.
f
D.C. al
CODA
accel. e cresc.
ff

Sun-Dance *

Lily Strickland

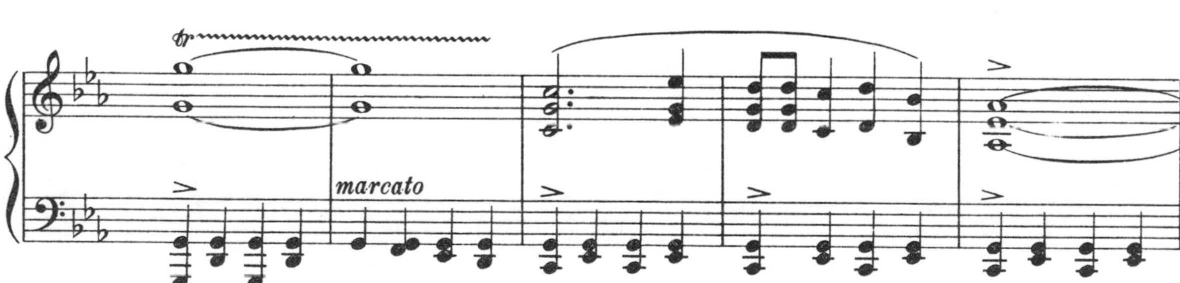

* The Cherokee Indians (habitat, the Blue Ridge in North and South Carolina) were sun-worshippers, and celebrated the rising sun with religious festivals at which they danced the sun dance. A remnant of this tribe still dwells in the Whitewater country, N. C.

f

sfz

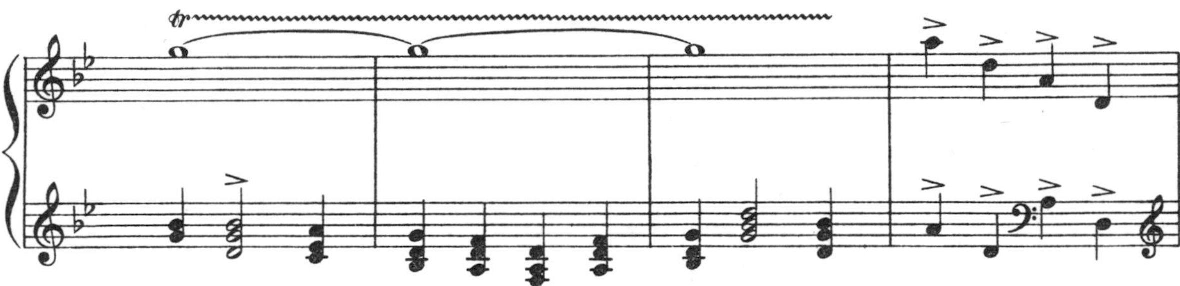
tr

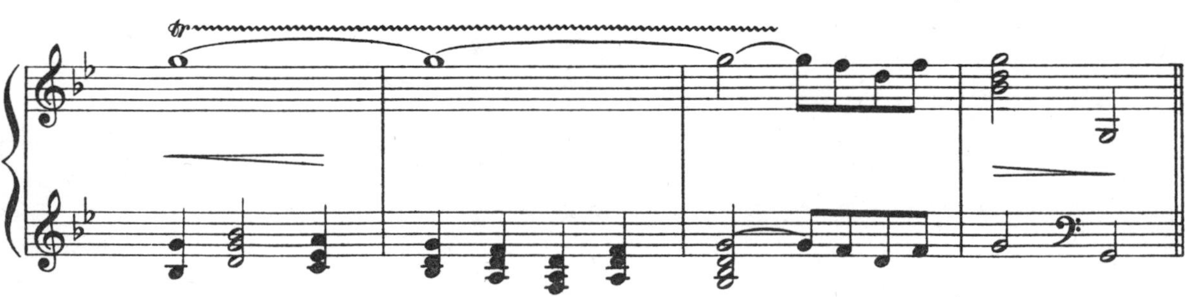
tr

pp
marcato
cresc.

ff poco accel.

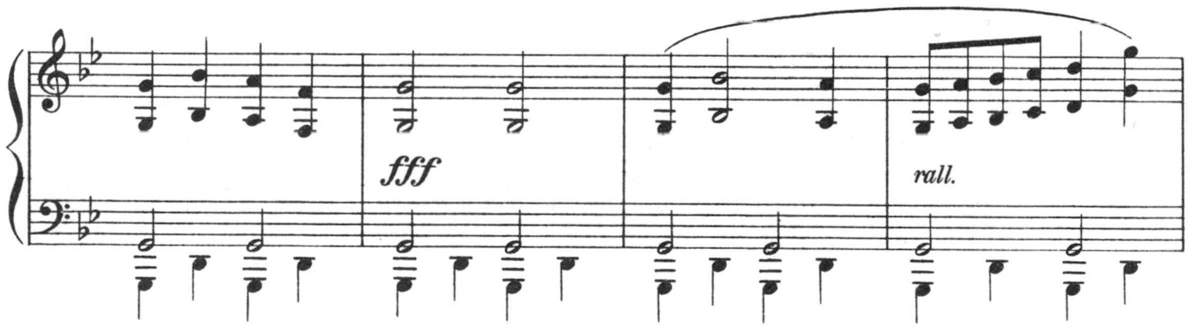
fff
rall.

marcato
poco a poco cresc.

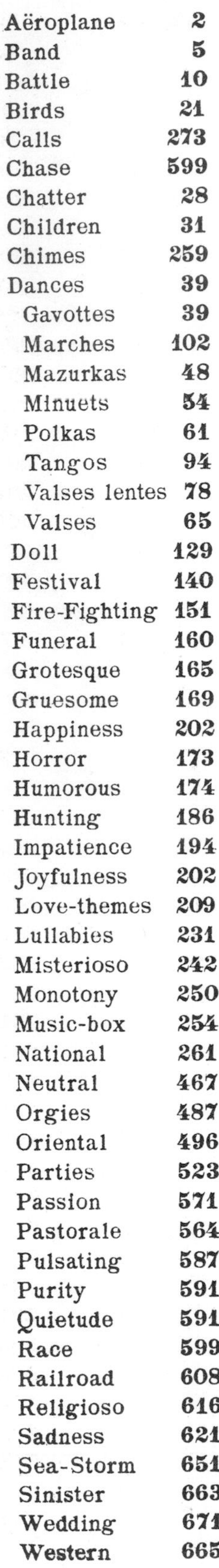

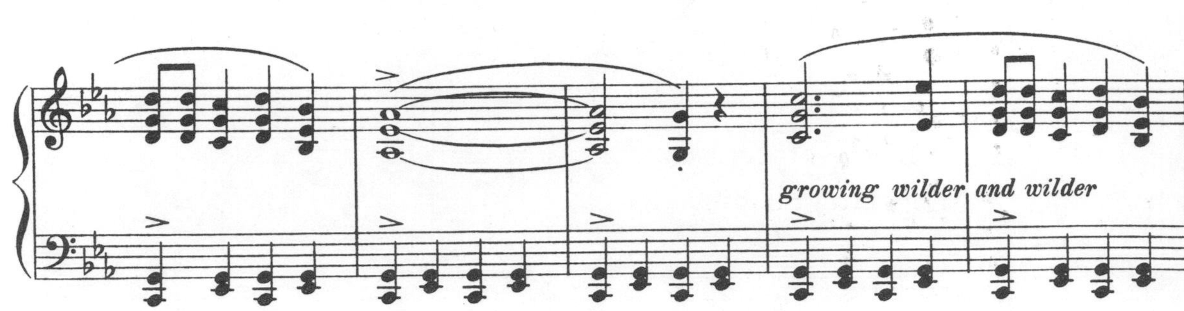
growing wilder and wilder

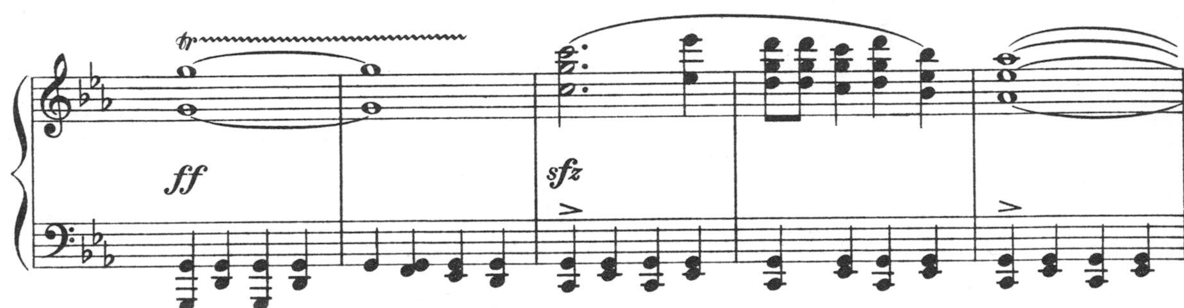
ff
sfz

sfz

fz
fff

Dance of the Young Maidens

Lily Strickland

Leggero grazioso

8

mp

f
rit.
Più vivo
p
cresc.
f
f

fp
fp
fp
fp
f
f cresc.
ff
rall.
più rall.
a piacere
pp

Tempo I°
pp
cresc.
cresc.
dim.
rall.
8
leggero
accel.

Garry Owen

College Hornpipe

Fisher's Hornpipe

Killarney

The Wearing o'the Green

Patriotic Air

St. Patrick's Day

National Song

24342

Fanfare e Marcia Reale

National Hymn

24342
31381

24342
31381

Garibaldi Hymn

Patriotic Air

24342

1.
2.
f
Fine
p
1.
2.
D. S. al Fine

"Maria, Marì!,,

"Marie, ah, Marie!"

Poem by Vincenzo Russo
English version by
Dr. Th. Baker

Eduardo di Capua

* Or: speranno d'a parlà.

Più mosso
mf
cresc.
Ah! Ma - ri - a, Ma - rì! Quan-ta suon-no che per-do pe te;
Ah, Ma - rie! ah, Ma - rie! All the sleep I am los-ing for thee!
mf
cresc.
p
3
rall.
a tempo
mf
Fam - m'ad - dur - mì, Ab-brac - cia-to un po-co cu te! Ah! Ma -
Now let me rest For a mo-ment a-sleep on thy breast! Ah, Ma -
3
a tempo
p
rall.
mf
cresc.
3
f
rì - a, Ma - rì! Quan-ta suon-no che per-do pe te; Fam - m'ad-dur-
rie! ah, Ma - rie! All the sleep I am los-ing for thee! Now let me
cresc.
3
f
1.2.
3.
mì, Oj Ma - rì! Oj Ma rì! rì!
rest, O Ma - rie, O Ma - rie! rie!

'O sole mio!

My Sunshine

Eduardo di Capua

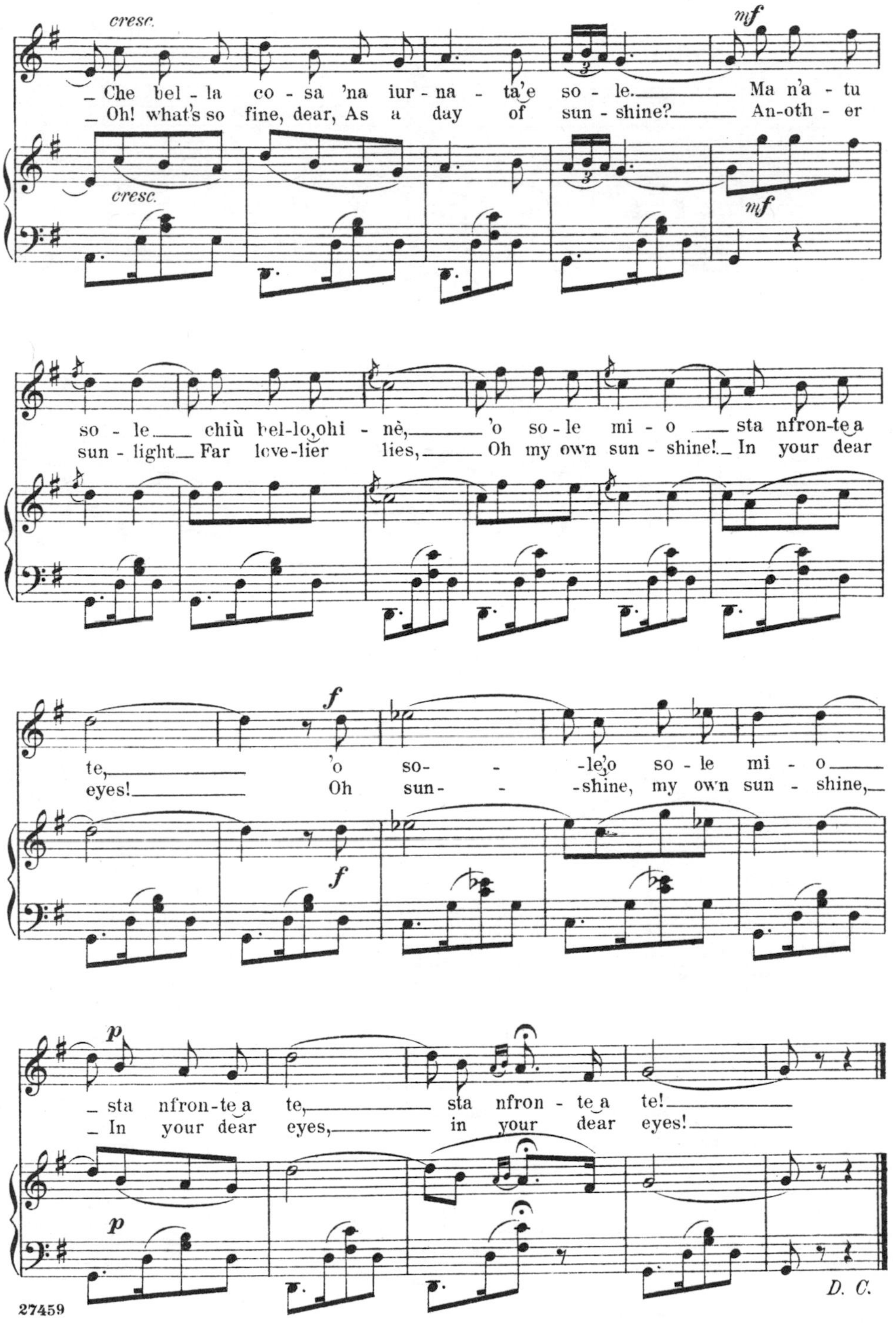

cresc. mf

_ Che bel-la co-sa 'na iur-na-ta'e so-le.___ Ma n'a-tu
_ Oh! what's so fine, dear, As a day of sun-shine?___ An-oth-er

so-le___ chiù bel-lo,ohi-nè,___ 'o so-le mi-o___ sta nfron-te a
sun-light___ Far love-lier lies,___ Oh my own sun-shine!_ In your dear

f

te,___ 'o so-le,'o so-le mi-o___
eyes!___ Oh sun-shine, my own sun-shine,_

p

_ sta nfron-te a te,___ sta nfron-te a te!___
_ In your dear eyes,___ in your dear eyes!___

D. C.

27459

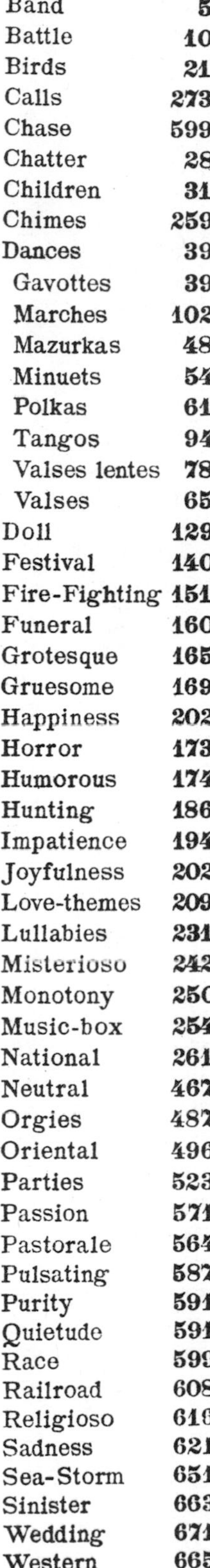

Venetian Boat-Song

F. Mendelssohn. Op. 30, No. 6

f
ff
sf
dimin.
pp
sf
dimin.
p
p
cresc. - - al - - f
dim.
p
cresc.
- al - - f
sf
dim.
sf
p
dim.
pp

Aëroplane 2
Band 5
Battle 10
Birds 21
Calls 273
Chase 599
Chatter 28
Children 31
Chimes 259
Dances 39
Gavottes 39
Marches 102
Mazurkas 48
Minuets 54
Polkas 61
Tangos 94
Valses lentes 78
Valses 65
Doll 129
Festival 140
Fire-Fighting 151
Funeral 160
Grotesque 165
Gruesome 169
Happiness 202
Horror 173
Humorous 174
Hunting 186
Impatience 194
Joyfulness 202
Love-themes 209
Lullabies 231
Misterioso 242
Monotony 250
Music-box 254
National 261
Neutral 467
Orgies 487
Oriental 496
Parties 523
Passion 571
Pastorale 564
Pulsating 587
Purity 591
Quietude 591
Race 599
Railroad 608
Religioso 616
Sadness 621
Sea-Storm 651
Sinister 663
Wedding 671
Western 665
398
Barcarolle
from "Tales of Hoffmann"
Moderato
J. Offenbach
pp
molto cantabile
21108

sempre più dolce
morendo
ppp

Tarentelle

Edited and fingered by
Louis Oesterle

Théodore Lack. Op. 20

p una corda
Con brio.
ff tre corde

f
p
pp
poco riten.
a tempo
p con grazia

pp
leggiero
pp una corda
f tre corde
f
p
pp
poco riten.
a tempo

20562
31381

dim. e poco riten.
a tempo
ff
ff e con
fuoco
Ped.

Mexico

National Song

31381

31381

Norway

Sönner af Norge

National Song

Walzer

Edvard Grieg. Op. 12, No. 2

Allegro moderato.

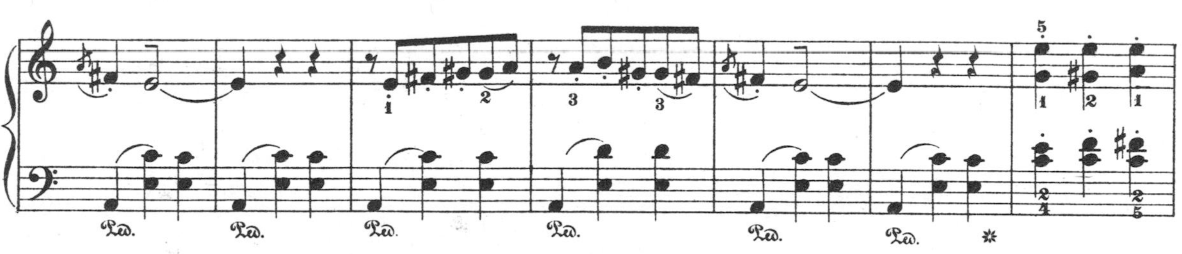

Printed in the U.S.A.

p
rit.
a tempo
rit.
f
pp
f rit.
p
Coda.
p dolce
pp

Norwegisch

Printed in the U. S. A.

fz
pp
ff
sempre rit.
Ped.

Norwegian Dance

Edited and fingered by
Adolf Ruthardt

Edvard Grieg. Op. 35, No. 2

15480

Printed in the U. S. A.

Allegro. (♩ = 112.)
tre corde
f stretto

Tempo I.
p dolce
p sempre
poco
una corda
a tempo
rit.
pp
sempre pp
poco rit. e morendo
ppp
una corda

Swedish Wedding March

A. Söderman. Op. 12

Arranged by Benno Scherek

Allegro e leggiero
Schnell und leicht

mf

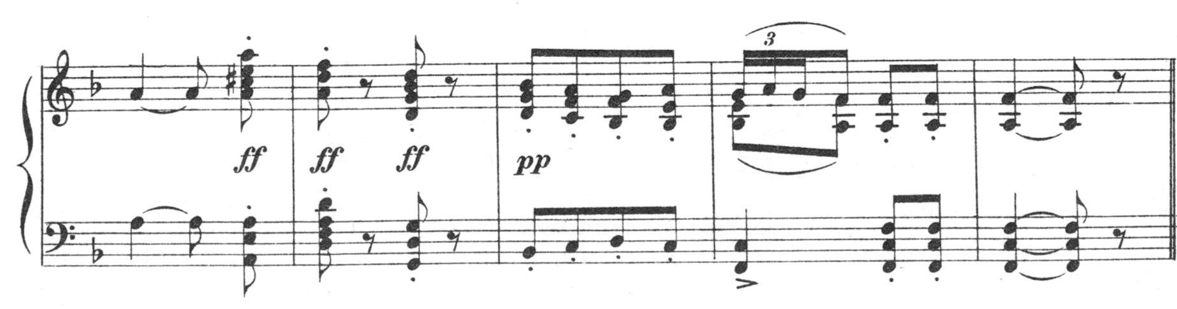

Printed in the U.S.A.

f
ff
ff
ff
ff
pp
mf
ff
ff
ff
ff
pp
Fine.

TRIO.

p
p
dolce.

f
p
dolce.
ff

ff marcato.
p

ff marcato.

pp
Marsch D. C. al Fine.

Poland's not yet dead in slavery

Patriotic Air

31381

Krakowiak

Danse Polonaise

E. Mlynarski. Op. 5, No. 1

23729
31381

tranquillo
legato
poco cresc.
dim.
poco cresc.
l.h.

rit.
a tempo
p
mf
cresc.
f
p
cresc.
mf
p e dim.
rit.
a tempo
dim.e
ritard. al Fine.
ppp

Portugal

National Hymn

Roumania

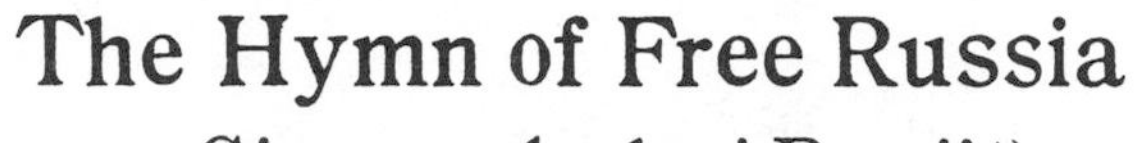

The Hymn of Free Russia

Gimn svobodnoi Rossii*)

March, 1917

Poem by
Konstantin Balmont
English version by
Vera and Kurt Schindler

Music by
Alexandre Gretchaninoff
Arranged and edited by
Kurt Schindler

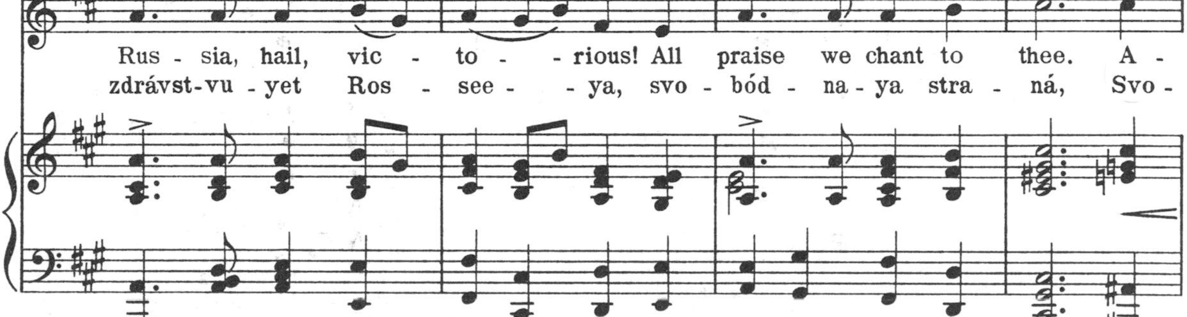

*) As the Russian language has several vowels and consonants not contained in the English language, the phonetic spelling has to use special devices to produce the exact sound. Thus *z* stands for soft s, *ee* for long i, as in feel, *kh* for the foreign ch, *zh* for the French j, as in "je, jamais," *oo* for the foreign long u, *ui* for a short French "oui."

ty - rant_ shall en - slave_ thee, Thy sun a - ris - es_
gōō - tsha - ya der - zhá - va, bez - brézh - nui o - kee -
f
bright; All_ hail to_ those who_ gave_ thee New_
án. Bor - tzám za vól - yu slá - va, raz -
ff
f
Free-dom's sa-cred light! Young Rus-sia, hail, vic - to - rious! All
vyé-yav-shim too - mán! Da zdrávst-vu-yet Ros - see - ya, svo -
ff
ff
ff

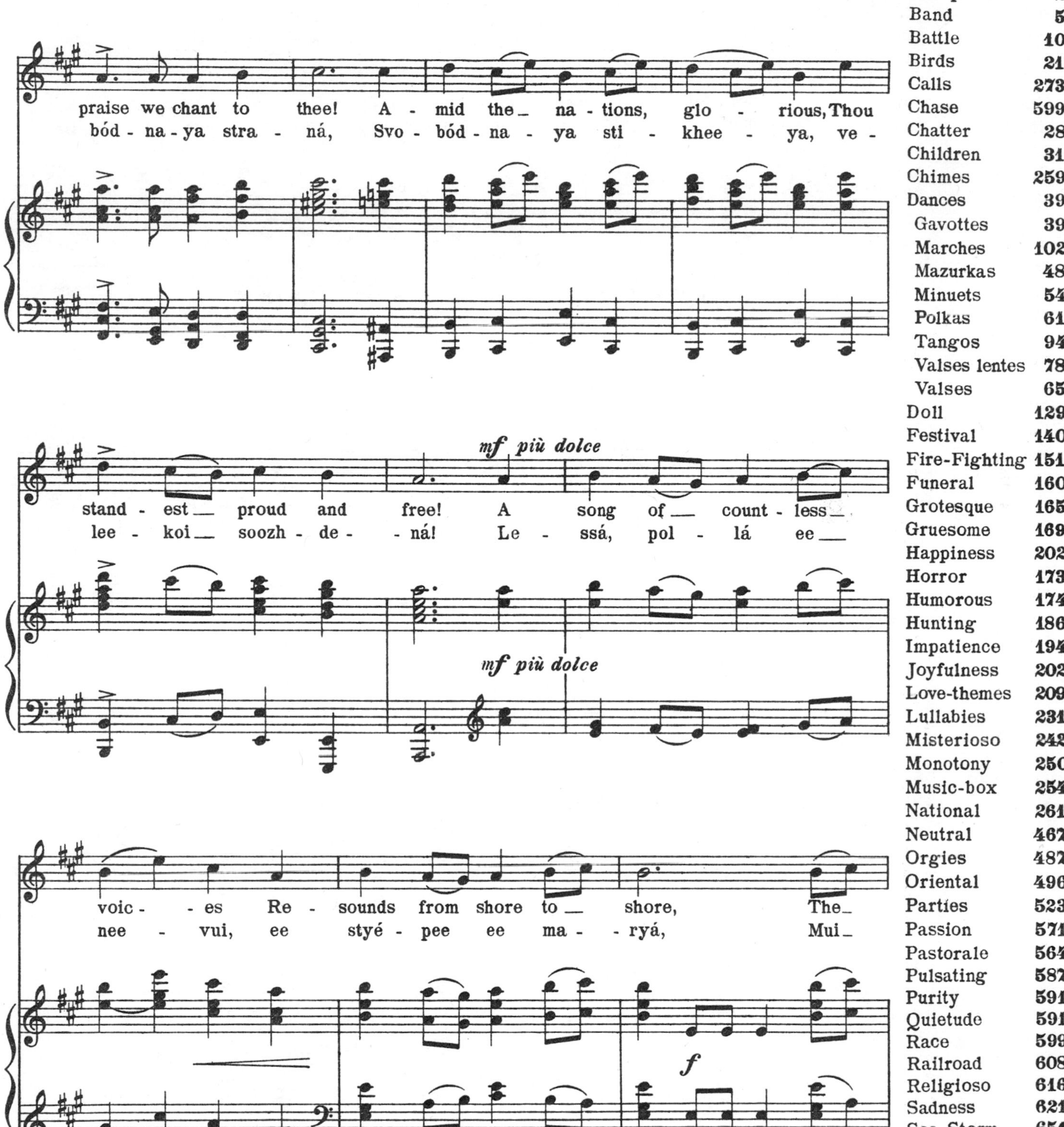
praise we chant to thee! A - mid the_ na - tions, glo - rious, Thou
bód - na - ya stra - ná, Svo - bód - na - ya sti - khee - ya, ve -
mf più dolce
stand - est_ proud and free! A song of_ count - less_
lee - koi_ soozh - de - - ná! Le - ssá, pol - lá ee_
mf più dolce
voic - - es Re - sounds from shore to_ shore, The_
nee - vui, ee styé - pee ee ma - ryá, Mui_
f

ff
Rus - sian folk re - joic - es With Free-dom ev - er - more. Young
vol - nui ee stchast - lee - vui, nam vsyem ga - reet za - ryá. Da
cresc.
ff
Rus - sia, hail, vic - to - - rious! All praise we chant to thee; A -
zdrávst - vu - yet Ros - see - - ya, svo - bód - na - ya stra - ná! Svo -
fff riten.
mid the_ na - tions, glo - rious, Thou stand - est_ proud and free!
bód - na - ya sti - khee - ya ve - lee - koi soozh - de - ná!
fff riten.

Kozácká ukolébavka

Cossack Lullaby

J. Jiránek.

23780

p
f
pp
p
mf
rit.
a tempo
l. h.
l. h.
pp
rit.
Ped.

Russian Dance

Rudolf Friml. Op. 83, No. 4

Printed in the U. S. A.

più animato
mf
cresc.
rit.
p tempo primo
cresc.
rit.

mf a tempo
accelerando
tr

marcato

cresc.

cresc.

f a tempo
cresc.
ff
Ped.

Vivace

24159
31381

f
ff
Ped.
cresc.
fff
marcatissimo

Vivacissimo
p
cresc. poco a poco
cresc. sempre
fff

Scotland

Auld Lang Syne

Folk-Song

24342

The Campbells are coming

National Song

Allegro marcato

The Bluebells of Scotland

National Song

Annie Laurie
Folk-Song
Andante
cresc.
p

Scots, wha hae wi' Wallace bled

National Song

Comin' Thro' the Rye

Srpska Narodna Himna

Serbian National Anthem

Words arranged by
Florence G. Attenborough

srp - ske brod. Bož - e spas - i Bož - i bran - - i
in - to light, Till our ship of State be an - chored
Srps - kog kral - ja, Srps - ki rod: Bož - e spas - i, Boš - e
Thro' the mer - cy of Thy might: Till our foes be spent and
bran - - i, Srps - kog kral - ja, Srps - ki rod.
scat - ter'd In the full - ness of the Light,
Srps-kog kral - ja, Srps - ki rod.
Ser - bia's king, and Ser - bia's land, Guard for ev - er more.
ff
ff

Spain

National Hymn

Spanish Dances

Revised and fingered by
Wm Scharfenberg

Moritz Moszkowski

Allegro brioso.

simile.

8ves ad lib.

mf

Ped.

ff
f
p e gra-
zioso.
Ped.

marcato.
8ves ad lib.
p
marcato.
8ves ad lib.
f
f

Moderato.
p con sentimento.
simile.
f
marc. un poco.
sfz
cresc.
sfz
sfz
sfz
pp
p con sentimento.

gajo.
con fuoco.
marcato.

p con sentimento.
simile.
f
marc. un poco.
sfz
cresc.
sfz
sfz
sfz
pp
p con sentimento.

Juanita

Spanish Ballad

Words by the
Hon. Mrs. Norton

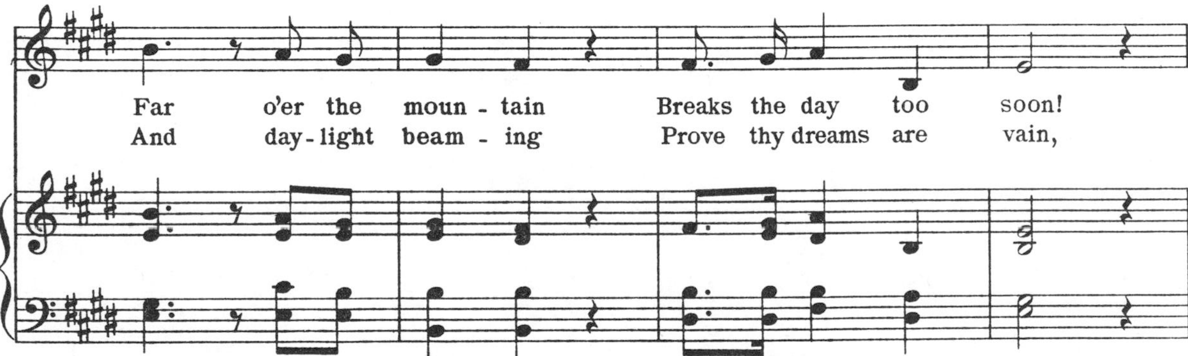

Meno mosso

Wear - y looks, yet ten - der__ Speak their fond fare - well!
In thy heart con - sent - ing__ To a prayer gone by?

a tempo *p*

Ni - ta! Jua - - ni - ta! Ask thy soul if we should part!
Ni - ta! Jua - - ni - ta! Let me lin - ger by thy side!

Estudiantina

Suite de Valses

Émile Waldteufel

INTRODUCTION.
Tempo di Valse.

VALSE.
ESTUDIANTINA. *(REFRAIN.)*

1.

Printed in the U. S. A.

ESTUDIANTINA. (COUPLET.)
2.
p espressivo.
Fine.
CHANSON D' AUTOMNE.
ff
p
ff
p
ff
D S

JOTA DE LA ESTUDIANTINA.

3.

f

1 2

p

Fine.

TIRANA.

1 2

f

D.S.

DE CADIZ AL PUERTO.

4.

EL TRIPILI.

CODA.
ff
mf
1
2

p
3
ff

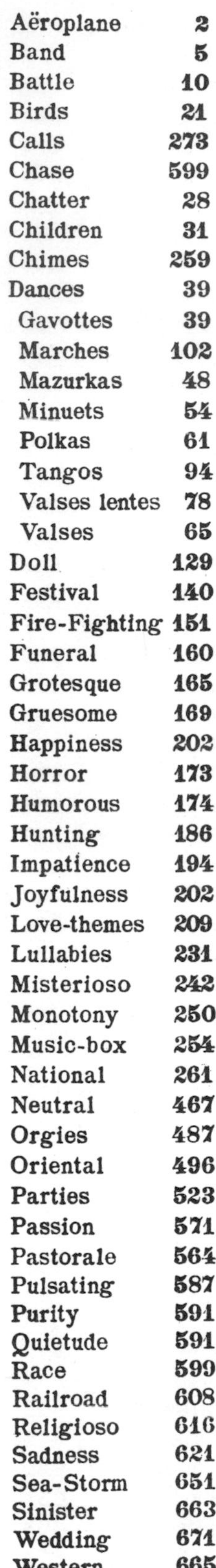

ff

Fine.

Uruguay

National Hymn

24342

f
p
poco accel.
p animato
3

Venezuela

National Hymn

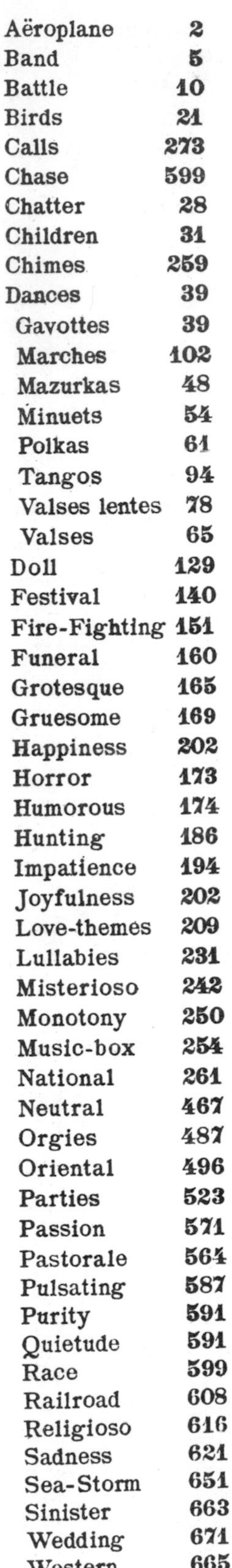

ff

D. S. al Fine

Wales

National Song

Molto animato

ff

coll' 8a bassa

1. 2.

24342

To my Friend Mr. Ralph Brigham

Radiance

Gatty Sellars

26674
31381

p
Ped.
Ped.
Ped.
Ped.
Ped.
Ped.

pp
cresc.
poco rit.
Ped.
Ped.
Ped.

a tempo
p
Ped.
Ped.
Ped.
Ped.
Ped.
Ped.

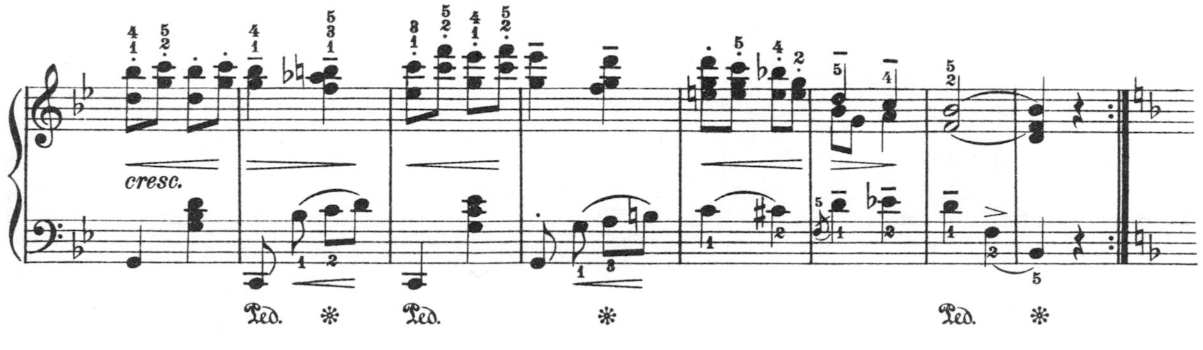
cresc.
Ped.
Ped.
Ped.

mf
Ped.
Ped.
Ped.
Ped. simile
a tempo
rit.
Ped.
Ped.
p
mf
Ped.

The Lotus Lake

Theodora Dutton

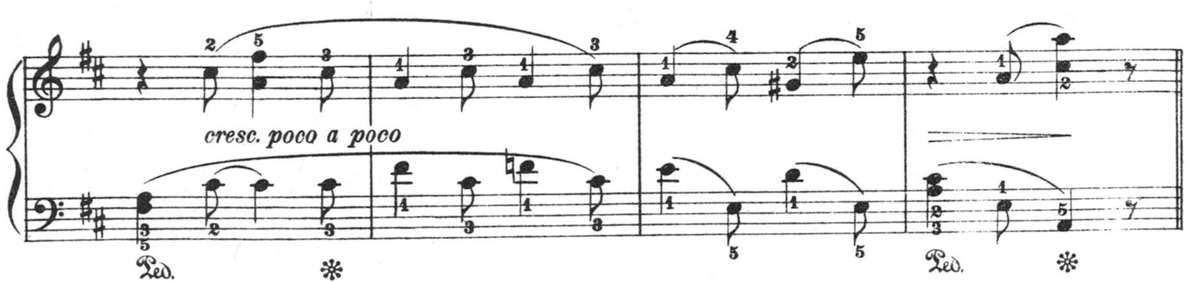

26863 c

sempre con moto ed espr.
mp
mf
mp dolce
p espressivo
cresc.
f
Tempo I°
mp

cresc.
Ped.
cresc.
Ped.
p
mp cresc.
Ped.
mp cresc.
Ped.
f
mp
pp

Albumblatt

Edvard Grieg. Op. 12, No. 7

Allegretto e dolce

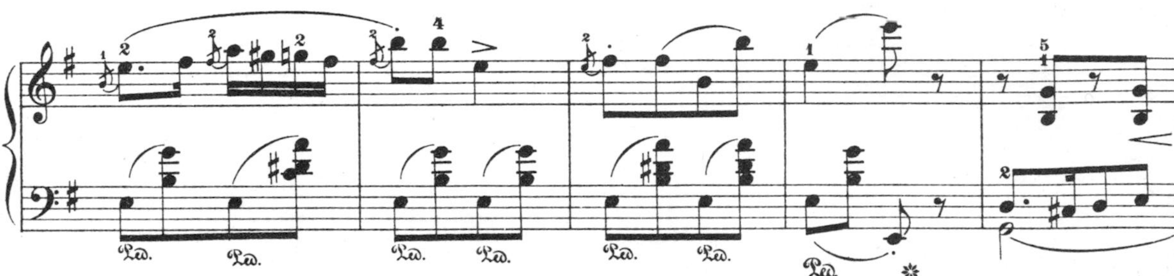

sosten.
fz
Ped.

Arabesque

Edited and fingered by
Max Vogrich

B. Wrangell. Op. 1, № 3.

Non Allegro

p legato possibile.

riten. poco.

p
mezza voce.

a tempo.

mf

riten. poco.

a tempo.

mezzo voce.

p

riten.

p

Printed in the U. S. A.

a tempo.
mf
f accel.
poco riten.
a tempo.
p
mezza voce.

riten.
mezza voce.
a tempo.
mf
accel.
Più mosso.
f marcato.
cresc.
poco a poco dim. e
ff
p
riten.
ppp

Edited and fingered by
G. Buonamici

Moments Musicaux

F. Schubert. Op. 94

Moderato. (♩= 96)

1.

cresc. *decresc.* *cresc.*

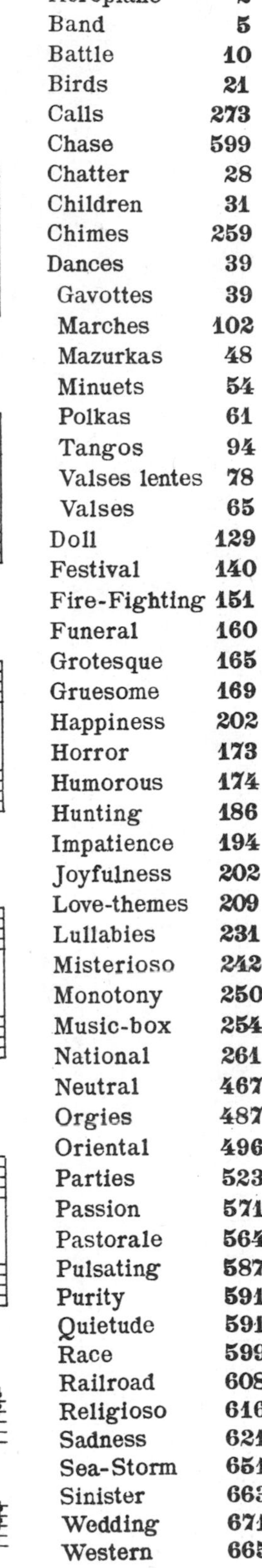

cresc.

pp

dimin.

p

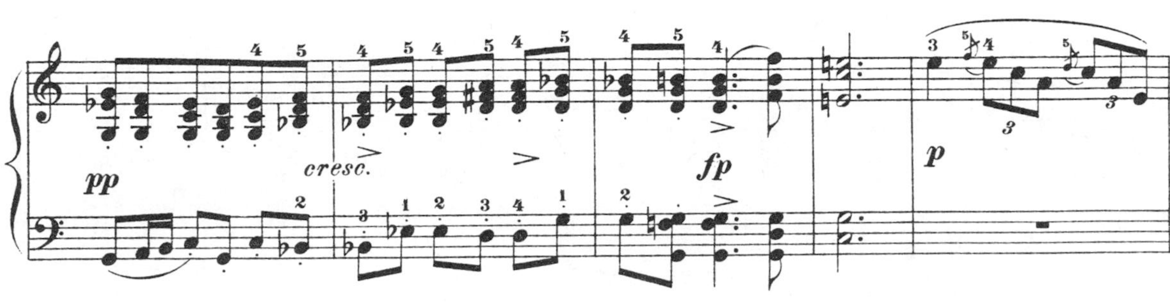
pp
cresc.
fp
p

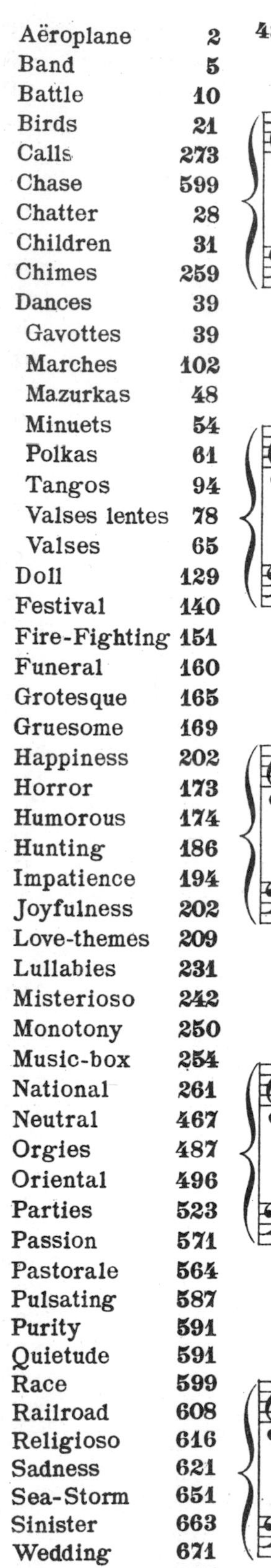

f sf sf sf sf 1

p decresc. pp

p

pp cresc. fp

Moments Musicaux

(No. 3)

Edited and fingered by
G. Buonamici

F. Schubert. Op. 94

3.

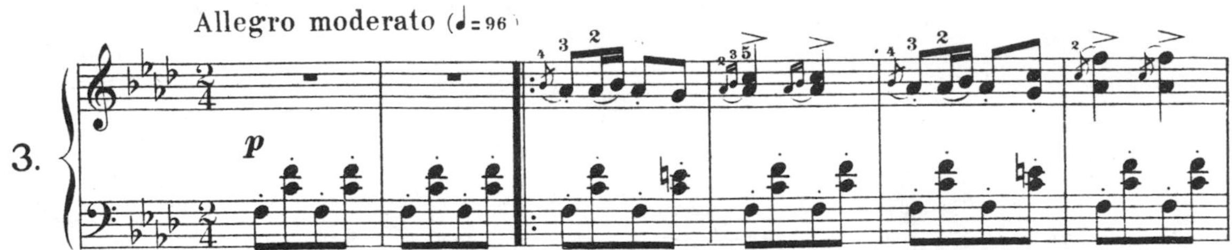

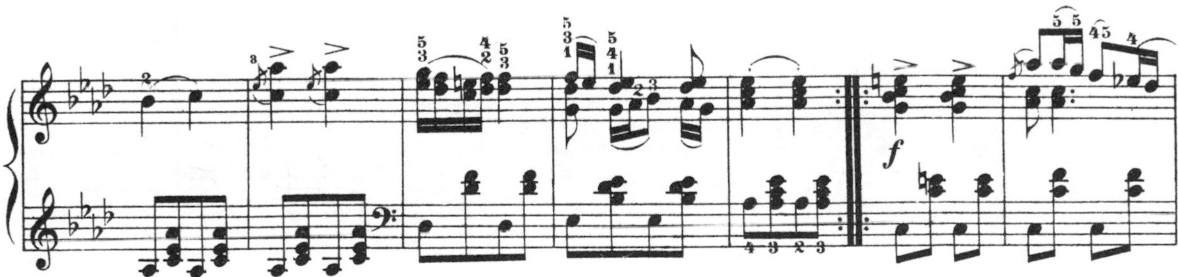

*) May also be played thus:

7150
31381

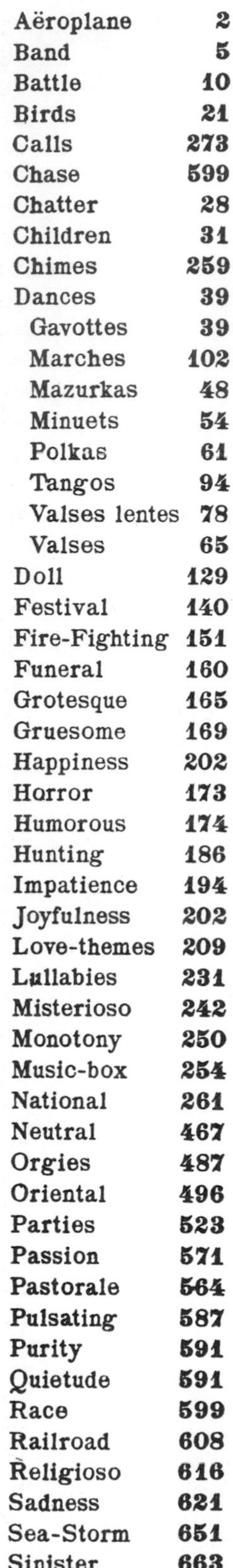

ppp

dimin.

dimin.

Chant sans Paroles

Moderato
Rudolf Friml. Op. 49
p legato

rit.
p a tempo

con passione
rit.
poco rit.

molto rit.

20232 C

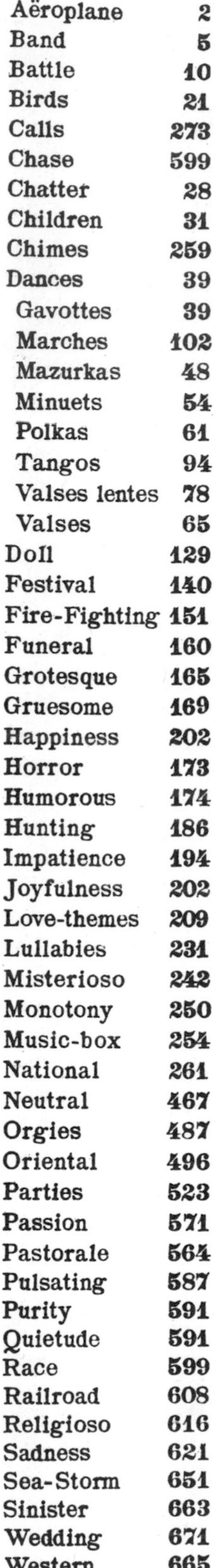

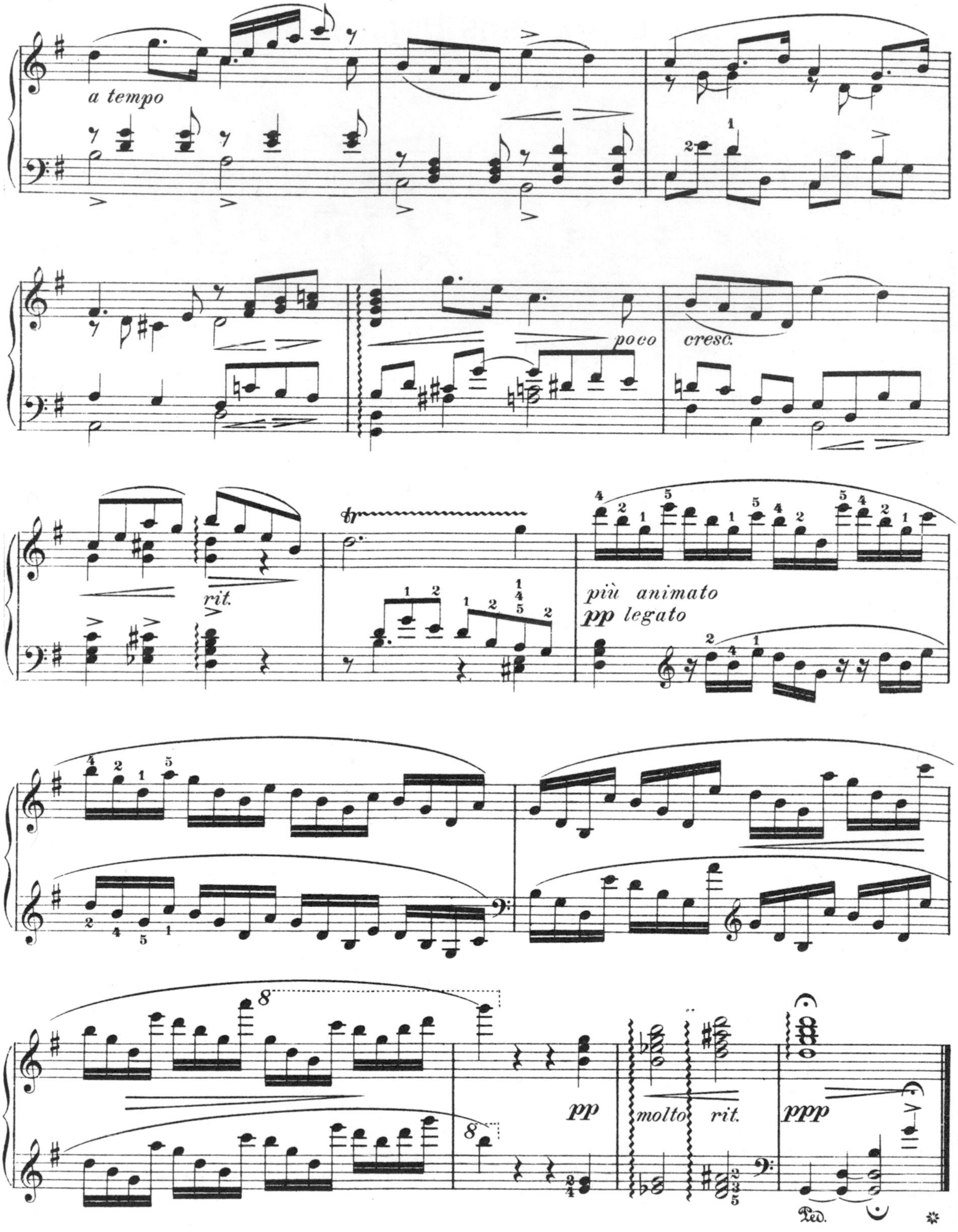

a tempo
poco cresc.
rit.
più animato
pp legato
pp
molto rit.
ppp
Ped.

20232

Fourth Movement
from l'Arlésienne Suite
Georges Bizet
Allegro assai e deciso
ppp
ppp
poco
a
poco
cresc.
sempre
cresc.
poco
a
poco

(54)
sempre
più
cresc.
ff

(54)
p
a
poco
a
poco
cresc.

mf
cresc.
f
molto
cresc.
fff

fff
fff

ff
fff
fff
fff fff fff fff fff fff fff

L'Automne et l'Hiver
Autumn and Winter

A. Glazounoff

sf
p cresc.
f
p
sf
p
sf
p cresc.
sf
mp
sf
mp
sf
mf
f
sf

Among the Arabs
Moderato (♩ = 68)
Otto Langey. Op. 158, No. 1
lamentoso
dim.

p
f
p
f
f
rit.
a tempo
f
mf

27005

dim.
pp
p
cresc.
molto rit.
a tempo
f
p cresc. ed accel.
f
poco a poco tornando al tempo

a tempo
ff
mf
f
mf
f
ff
dim.
Più lento
p dolce
espress.
f
poco riten.
a tempo
sfz dim.
p
morendo
pp

27005
31361

Morris Dance

mf
p
cresc.
f
tr

Molto sostenuto
mf
mf
mf
f
mf

f
mf
f
5
5
5
5
mf

Vers l'Oasis
In Sight of the Oasis
Maurice Baron
Tempo di Marcia molto moderato ♩= 66
ppp
pp
pp
cresc.
p
mf
cresc. poco a poco
f
ff

ff
Più lento ♩= 58
p
pp grazioso
8

8
p
poco rit.
pp a tempo

8
Tempo I°
ff
dim.
mf
5
dim.
Più moderato
p religioso
sempre dim.
ppp
perdendosi

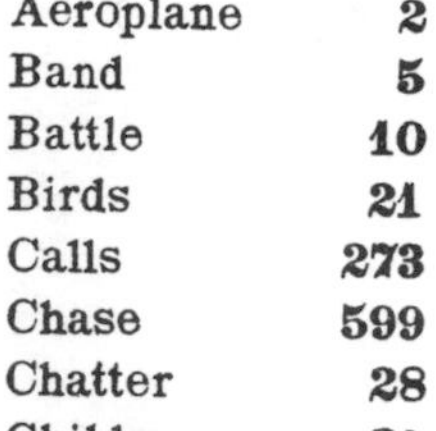

Arab Dance

Edvard Grieg

Allegretto vivace

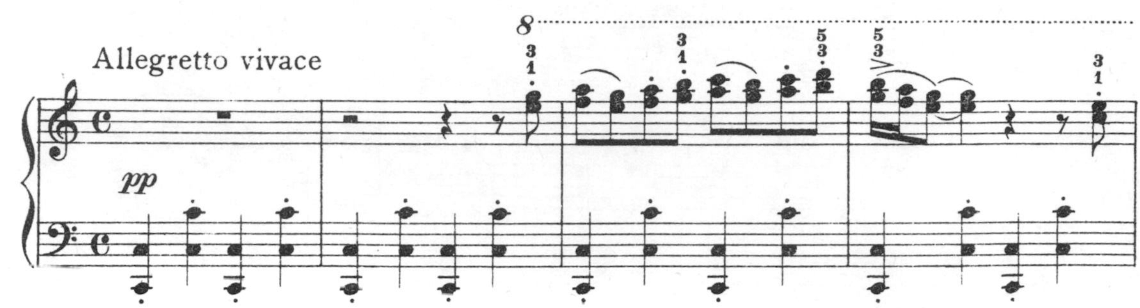

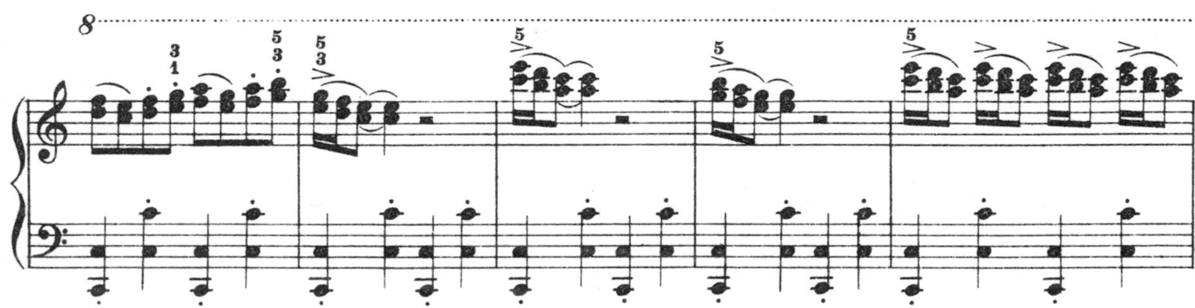

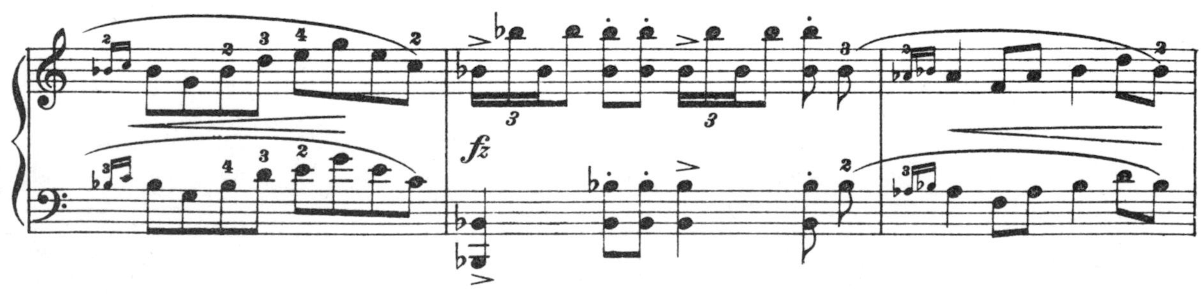

fz
ff
p
sempre p
Ped.

poco rit.
a tempo
cresc.
f
Ped.

dim.
p
dolce
fp
fp
p

29690
31381

fz
Ped.
ff
p
sempre p

sempre p
Ped.

Ped.

tr
f
p
Ped.

tr
f
Ped.

fz
Ped.
fz
ff
sempre ff
p
dim.
pp

First Movement of
l'Arlésienne Suite

Georges Bizet

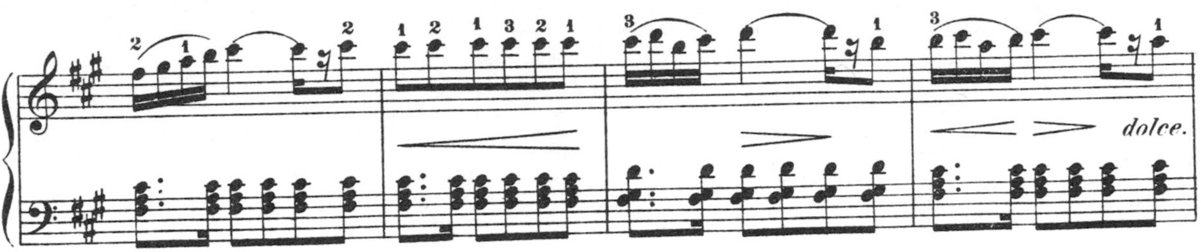

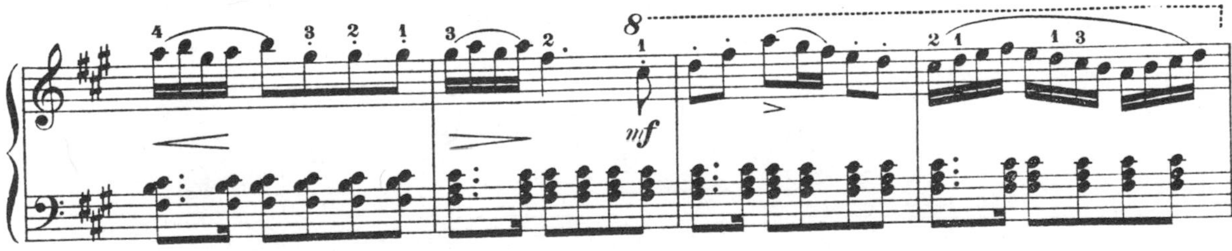

31381

8
sf
un
poco più p
f
dim.
dolce.
f
mf
(45)
(45)

(348)
cresc.
(148)
dim.
D. C.

Vanity

Caprice

Ralph C. Jackson

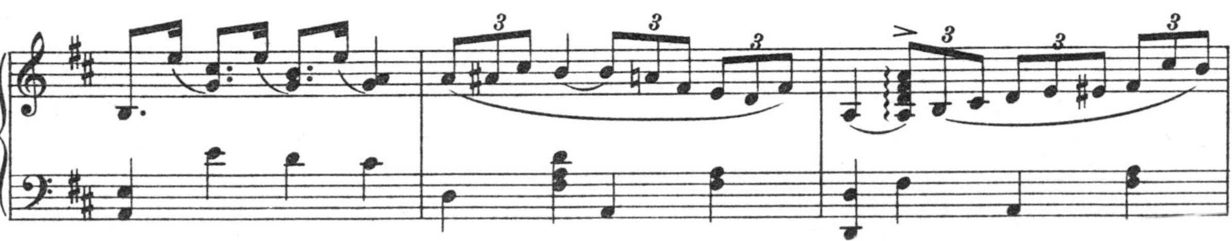

Printed in the U. S. A.

fz
fz
fz
fz
p
ten.
rall.
Tempo I

mf

rall.
a tempo
1.
2.
f
rall.

Idilio

Edited and fingered by
Louis Oesterle

Théodore Lack. Op. 134

20562

poco
a poco cresc.
f
dim. e rall.
p
mf
p
mf
p rit.
8
pp delicatamente
pp
l.h.
rall.
Ped.
20362

Scarf-Dance

Scène de Ballet

Revised and fingered by
W<u>m</u> Scharfenberg

C. Chaminade

p delicatamente
f
p
dim.
pp
cresc.
f
dim.
p
pp rubato
cresc.
f
dim.
p
pp

p delicatamente
p
dim.
pp
cresc.
f
dim.
p
pp rubato
cresc.
f
dim.
p
pp
rit.
f secco

Souvenir

Piano Arrangement by
Andor Pintér

Franz Drdla

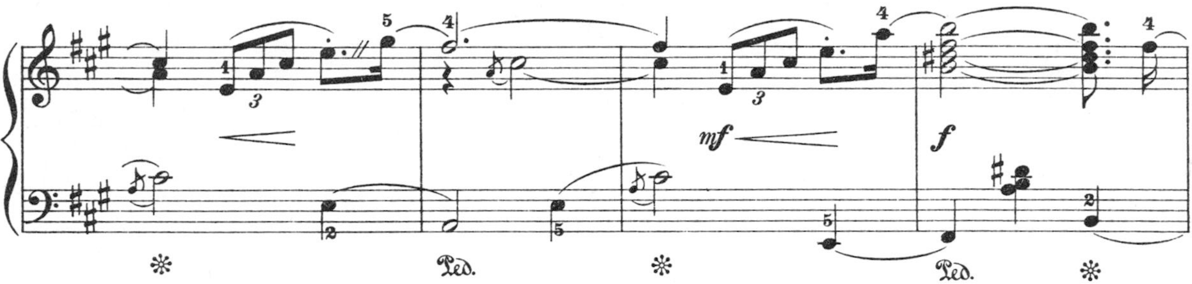

26402

a tempo
rit.
Più animato

pp
f
dim.
rit.
a tempo
pp
pp
p

animando poco a poco
cresc.
più largamente
dim.
p
cresc.
mf
f rit.
Tempo I°

mf
f
pp
p
mf
f
rit.
Meno
p
f
poco rit.
p
Presto
f
p
mf
rit.
mp

Pizzicati

Sylvia Ballet

Revised and fingered by
Wm Scharfenberg

Léo Delibes

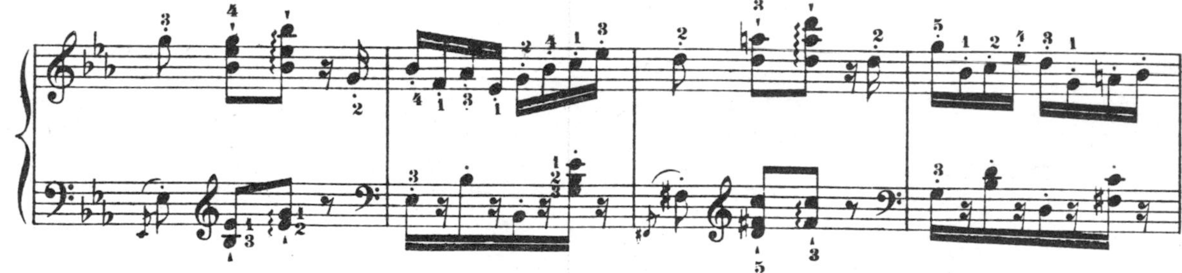

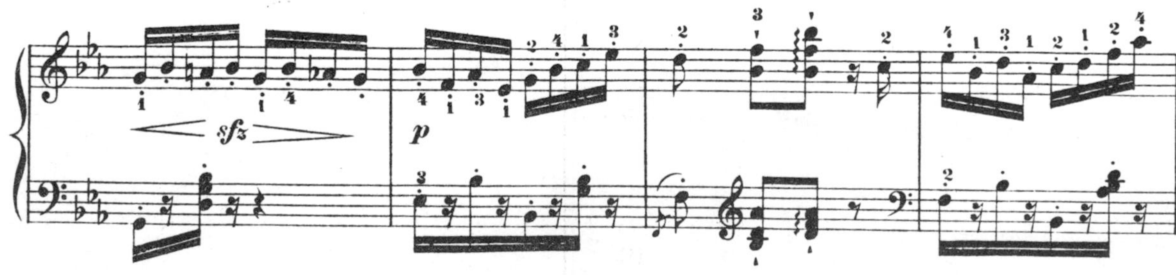

cresc.
mf
p
ten.
ten.
sfz
p
cresc.
mf

p
ben sostenuto.
p
ten.
ten.
ten.
ten.

più animato.
p
sfz
p
accel.
ten.
molto cresc.-
ten.
ff

Sérénade Badine

Edited and fingered by
Wm Scharfenberg

Gabriel-Marie

12143

pp
rit.
a tempo.
p
rit.
a tempo.
p
mf
poco rall.
a tempo.
p
mf
rit.

Un poco più animato.
mf
poco rit.
a tempo.
sf
p
cresc.
Poco animato.
sf
rit.
a tempo.
pp

Tempo I.
sf
accel.
rit.
p
sf
mf
a tempo.
poco rall.
p
a tempo.
mf
rit.
mf
a tempo.
pp
rit.
p

a tempo.
rit.
p
a tempo.
mf
poco rall.
p
mf
Calmato.
rit.
p
a tempo.
rit.
p leggiero.
pp

Serenata

Revised and fingered by
Wm Scharfenberg

M. Moszkowski. Op. 15, No. 1

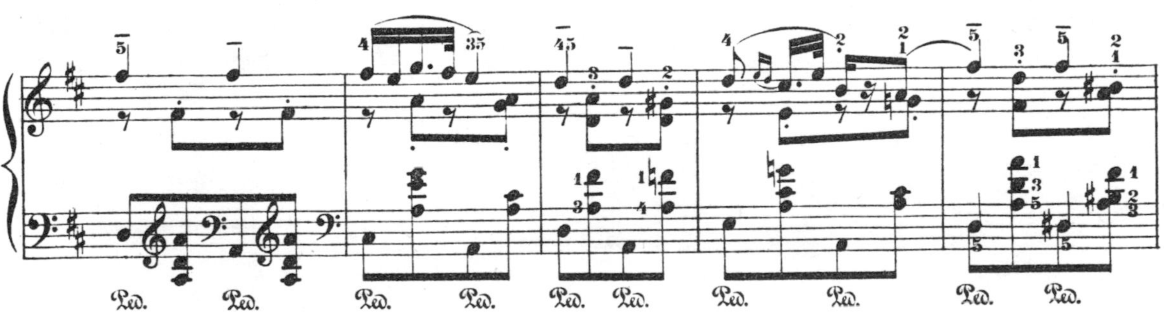

rinfz.
mp
cresc.
sfz
f
dimin.
molto ritard.
pp

a tempo
riten.
marc.
pp
un poco

To Master Harry Allen

"Ladies' faces, ribbons and laces"

Old-time Gavotte

cresc.
mf
Ped.
f
dim.
p

p
cresc.
p
cresc.
p

Spring Song

Allegretto grazioso (♩= 88)

F. Mendelssohn. Op. 62, No. 6

25496

a) The letters *o.* and *u.* indicate where the left hand is best placed over *(o.)* and under *(u.)* the right.

dimin.
grazioso
Ped. come sopra
cresc.
al
dim.

f
dimin.
p
cresc.
p dolce
cresc.
p dolce
grazioso
dimin.
pp
leggiero
Ped.ten.

Chant sans paroles

Song without words

Revised and fingered by Wm. Scharfenberg

P. Tschaikowsky

Printed in the U. S. A.

m.g.
m.g.
dim.
poco rit.
Tempo I
marcato
energico
cresc.

ff
dim.
p
f
cresc.
ff
dim.
p
p
sempre di - mi - nu - en - do
marcato la melodia
pp
ppp

Salut d'amour
Love's Greeting

Edited and fingered by
Louis Oesterle

Edward Elgar. Op.12

18094r

cresc.
a tempo
pp
p dolce
rit.
ppp
f
mf
cresc. molto
sf dim.
dim.
rit. pp

a tempo
poco string.
pp
Tempo I
rit.
pp
cresc.
p
cresc.
dim.
pp
cresc.

accel.
stacc.
cresc. molto
largamente
ff rit.
p rit.
pp l.h.
Tempo più lento
più lento
rit.
a tempo
pp rall. e dim.

14300 r
31881

f
Ped.
più f
ff
l.h.
p
molto

ff
p
ff
p
p
molto
ff
p
dim. e tranquillo
pp
dim. e tranquillo

tranquillo
pp
p
dim.
più tranquillo
pp
poco rit.
Ped.

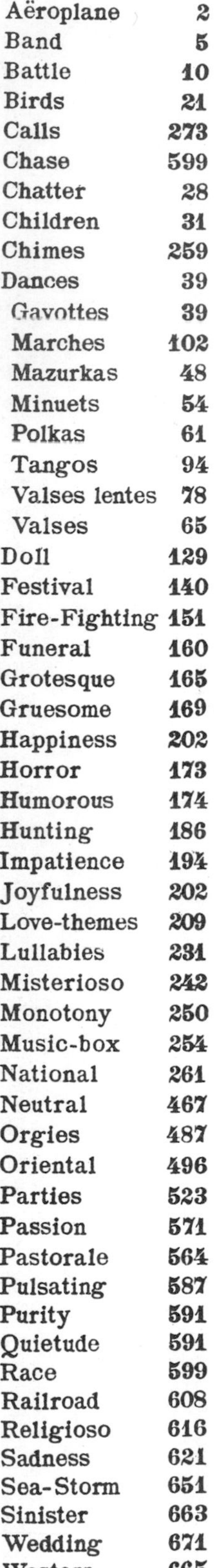

Fourth Movement

from l'Arlésienne Suite

Georges Bizet

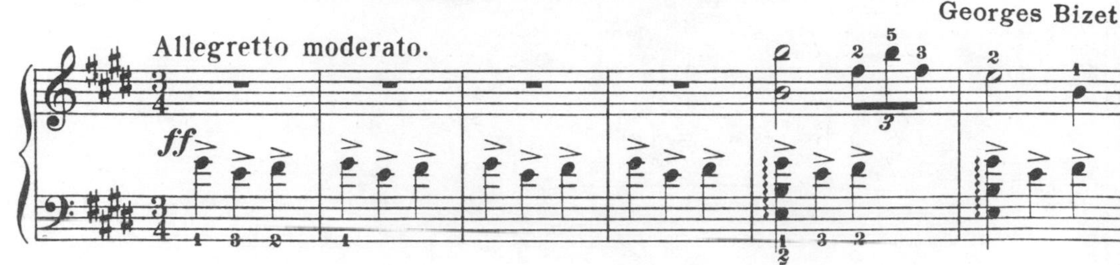

ff
ff
ff
pp
D. C.

First Movement of
l'Arlésienne Suite II

Edited and fingered by
W. K. Bassford

Georges Bizet

Valzer Appassionato

Theodora Dutton

la melodia ben cantando

a tempo
mp cresc. poco a poco
rit.
a tempo
espressivo
mp
cresc.
rubato
mp
rit.
a tempo
mp
molto espressivo

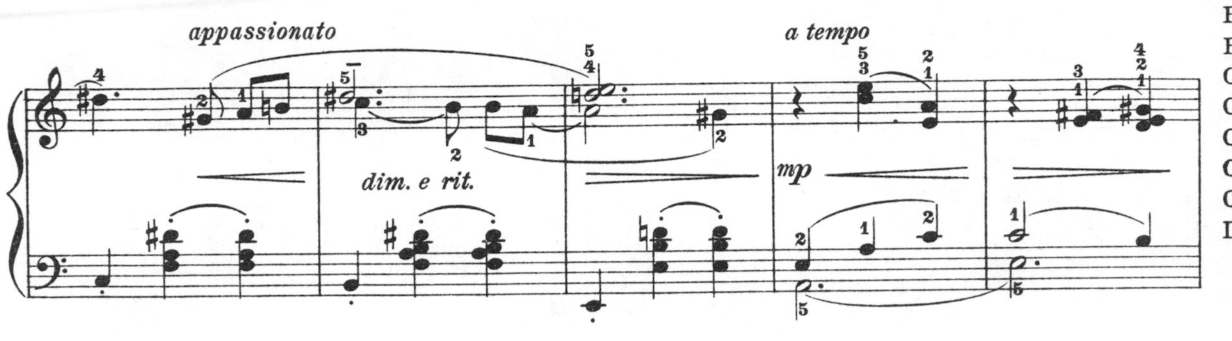
appassionato
a tempo
dim. e rit.
mp

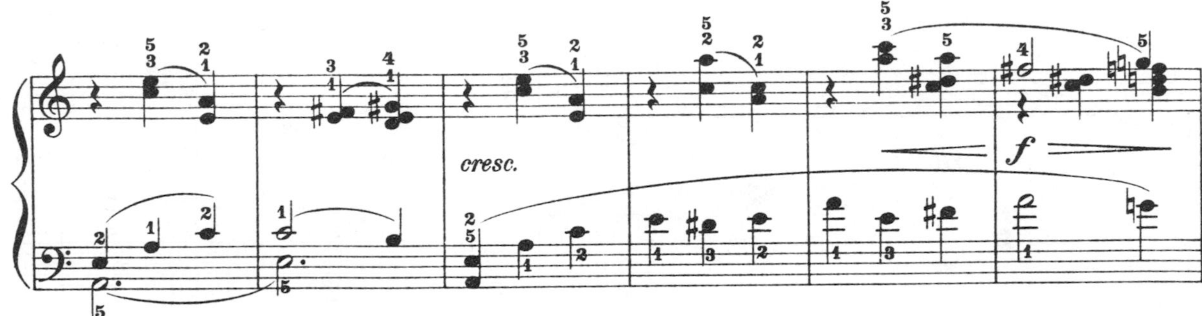
cresc.
f

mf
cresc. poco a poco

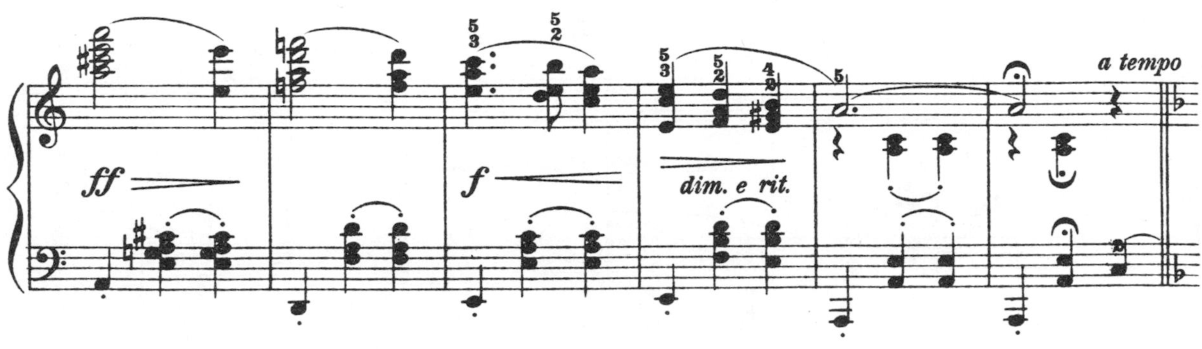
a tempo
ff
f
dim. e rit.

Con moto
con amore
rubato
cresc. poco a poco
f
la melodia ben cantando
a tempo
rit.
mp
cresc. poco a poco
f
dim. e rit.
a tempo
p
cresc. poco a poco
a tempo
a tempo
f rit.
rit.
mp

cresc. poco a poco
f rit.
a tempo
a tempo
mp grazioso
mp
scherzando
stringendo
f
f > mp

appassionato
cresc. poco a poco
rubato
f
a tempo
rit.
mp
cresc. poco a poco
f un poco rit.
a tempo
scherzando
p
un poco rit.
D. C.

Song without Words

Lost Happiness

Allegro non troppo

F. Mendelssohn. Op. 38, No. 2

cresc.
f
sf
f
sf
p
cresc.
f
dim.
p

Song without Words
Homeless

F. Mendelssohn. Op. 102, No. 1

a) Special attention should be given to the strict maintainance of this very original rhythm.

25496
31361

cresc.

p
cresc.
f
dimin.
p
dimin.
sempre Pedale

An den Frühling

To Spring

Allegro appassionato. (♩. = 84.) Edvard Grieg. Op. 43, No. 6

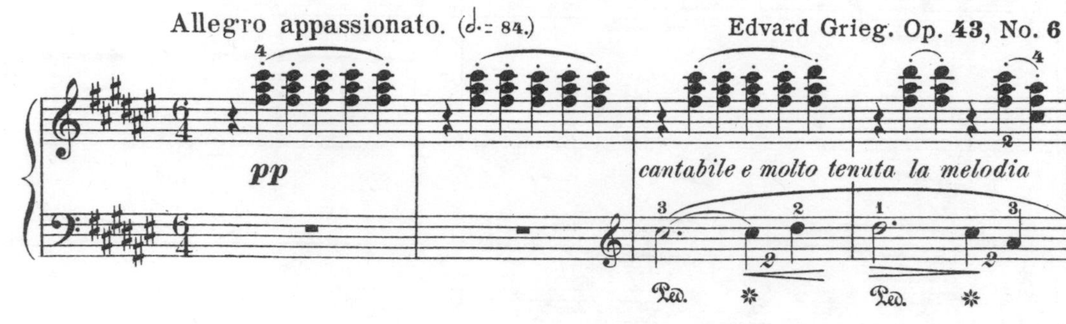

pp
fz rit. molto
p a tempo
cresc.
poco ritard.
f
p a tempo
stretto poco a poco

cresc.
r.h.
f agitato
f
più f
ritard.
ff
Tempo I.
p e dolce
p
Ped.

animato
poco rit.
a tempo
cresc.
poco rit.
a tempo
dim.
cresc.
dim.
15543

cresc. molto
f
sosten.
ritard.
ff
p a tempo
una corda
dim. e rit. poco a poco
pp a tempo
ritard.
r.h.
l.h.
piu rit.
Lento.
ppp
15543

Repose
Quiétude
Song without Words

Edited and fingered by
Louis Oesterle

Tempo moderato molto espressivo

Louis Gregh. Op. 53

l.h.
cresc. string.
dim.
p
con anima
string. molto cresc.
mf
l.h.
l.h.
sempre animato
f
dim.
a tempo
poco rit.
mf
cresc.
animato
f
20699

appassionato
poco rit.
a tempo
dolce
una corda
20699

tre corde
mf armonioso
marcato il canto
dimin. poco rit.
a tempo
cresc. molto
allargando
a tempo

20699

Third Movement of
l'Arlésienne Suite

Georges Bizet

Le Soir

Eventide

Allegretto moderato e cantabile. Ludvig Schytte. Op. 12, No. 3

poco a poco rit. - - - a tempo
f
p
sempre dimin.
una corda
pp
rit.
ppp
8

Song without Words
Faith
Andante (♩= 72)
F. Mendelssohn. Op. 102, No. 6
mf
cresc.
sf
dim.
p
cresc.
f
dim.
p
sf
f
p

25496
31381

Träumerei

R. Schumann. Op. 15, No. 7

Serenade

Edited and fingered by
Louis Oesterle

Ole Olsen. Op. 19, No. 2

Andante

Allegro No. 1

(A joyful crowd, pursuit, races, *etc.*)

Adolf Minot

Allegro

f

D.S.

Galop
Leichtes Blut

Johann Strauss. Op. 319

Trio.
Dal al Segno, poi Coda.
Coda.

Galop
Die Bajadère

Johann Strauss. Op. 351

13523

Trio.
f
sf
ff
ff
ff
f
1.
2.
f
p
f
D.C. al Segno ⊕, poi Coda
Coda.
p
cresc.
mf
sf

Cascaden-Galop

H. Herrmann. Op. 24

cresc.
f
f
1
2
ff
Trio.
p
mf
1
2
p
f
1
2
p

Finale
cresc.

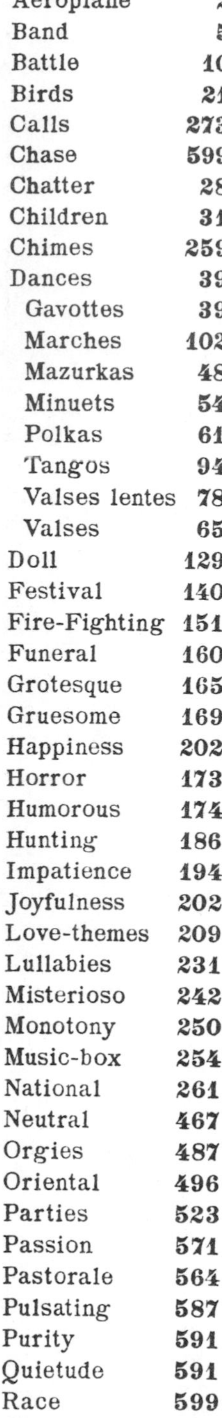

The Mill

Die Mühle

A. Jensen

Tranquillamente

Printed in the U. S. A.

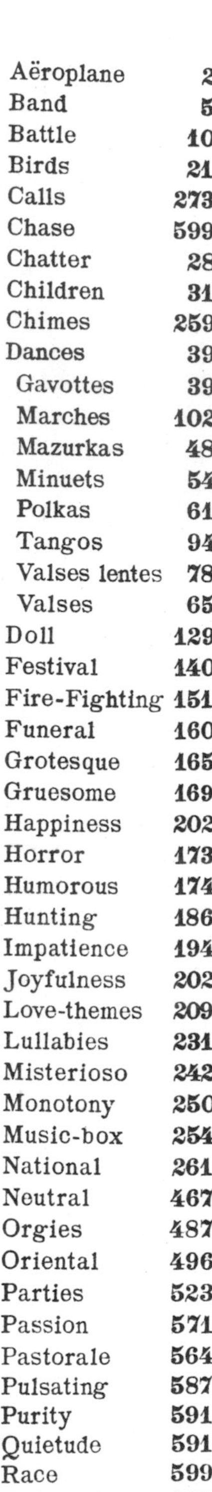

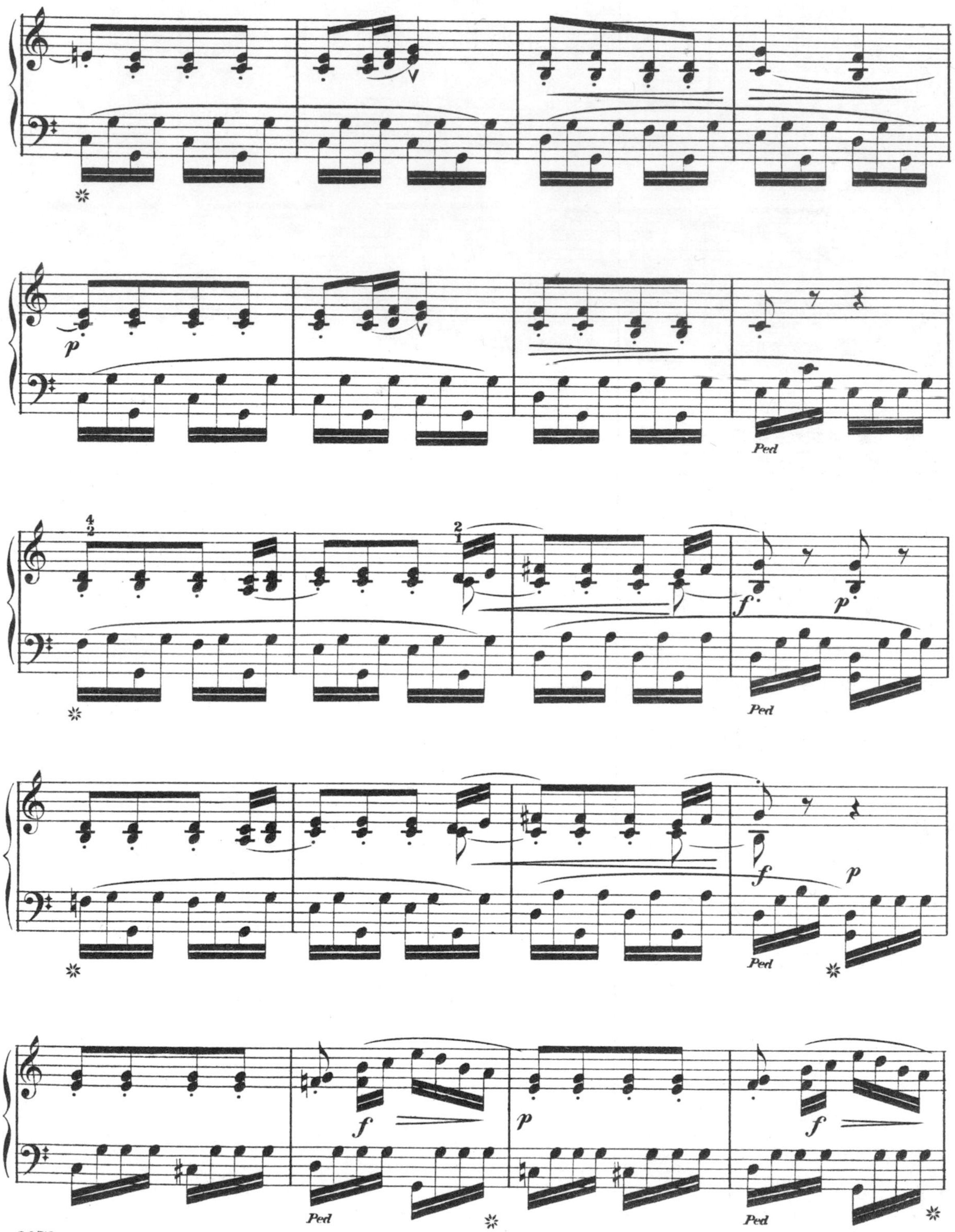

p
f
Ped
mf
pp
dim.
ppp

Spinning-Song

from the Opera

The Flying Dutchman

R. WAGNER

Revised and fingered by
Wm Scharfenberg

Josef Löw

21381

Largo

G. F. Händel

Transcribed by A. R. Parsons

Printed in the U. S. A.

M. D.
Ped
cresc.
ff
p
cresc.
f
Ped
mf
Ped
ff
Ped
p
Ped

cresc
f
ff
pp
ff
ff
fff
1927

The Old Hundredth
Isaac Watts
L. Bourgeois
(♩= 76)
f
cresc.
1. From all that dwell be - low the skies Let the Cre-at-or's praise a - rise! Let
2. E - ter-nal are Thy mer-cies, Lord, And truth e - ter-nal is Thy word: Thy
f
ff
the Re-deem-er's Name be sung Thro' ev-'ry land, by ev-'ry tongue.
praise shall sound from shore to shore Till suns shall rise and set no more. A - men.
Onward, Christian Soldiers
S. Baring-Gould
"St. Gertrude"
A. S. Sullivan
(♩= 108)
f
1. Onward, Christian sol-diers, Marching as to war, With the cross of Je-sus
f
mf
Go-ing on be - fore! Christ, the roy-al Mas-ter, Leads a-gainst the foe;
mf
ff
Forward in-to bat - tle, See, His banners go. Onward, Christian sol - diers,
Marching as to war, With the cross of Je - sus Go-ing on be-fore! A-men.

Aëroplane	2
Band	5
Battle	10
Birds	21
Calls	273
Chase	599
Chatter	28
Children	31
Chimes	259
Dances	39
Gavottes	39
Marches	102
Mazurkas	48
Minuets	54
Polkas	61
Tangos	94
Valses lentes	78
Valses	65
Doll	129
Festival	140
Fire-Fighting	151
Funeral	160
Grotesque	165
Gruesome	169
Happiness	202
Horror	173
Humorous	174
Hunting	186
Impatience	194
Joyfulness	202
Love-themes	209
Lullabies	231
Misterioso	242
Monotony	250
Music-box	254
National	261
Neutral	467
Orgies	487
Oriental	496
Parties	523
Passion	571
Pastorale	564
Pulsating	587
Purity	591
Quietude	591
Race	599
Railroad	608
Religioso	616
Sadness	621
Sea-Storm	651
Sinister	663
Wedding	671
Western	665

Lead, Kindly Light

To Mr. Alexander Raab

Romance

cresc.
f
mf espressivo
p con duolo
mf

sfz
sfz
f poco stretto
cresc.
ff grandioso
cresc.
fff
Ped.

dim.
pesante
rall.
mf
poco a poco più tranquillo
p
pp

First Movement of

Sonata quasi una Fantasia

Op. 27, No. 2

a) It is evident that the highest part, as the melody, requires a firmer touch than the accompanying triplet-figure; and the first note in the latter must never produce the effect of a doubling of the melody in the lower octave.

b) A more frequent use of the pedal than is marked by the editor, and limited here to the most essential passages, is allowable; it is not advisable, however, to take the original directions *sempre senza sordini* (i. e., without dampers) too literally.

11617

una corda.
pp
marcato, ma sempre p
cresc.
dimin.
p una corda.
p
pp
il basso sempre ten.

a) The player must guard against carrying his hand back with over-anxious haste. For, in any event, a strict pedantic observance of time is out of place in this period, which has rather the character of an improvisation.

11617
81381

a) The notes with a dash above them may properly be dwelt upon in such a way as to give them the effect of suspensions, e. g., : in fact, a utilization of the inner parts, in accordance with the laws of euphony and the course of the modulation, is recommended throughout the piece.

11617
31381

Prélude

25454

Prélude

Edited and fingered by
Rafael Joseffy

F. Chopin. Op. 28, No. 20

Elegie

Edvard Grieg. Op. 47, No. 7

Printed in the U. S. A.

poco mosso
espress.
cresc. ed
agitato
f
rit.
Tempo I.
p
morendo
pp

Berceuse

Armas Järnefelt
Transcribed by Erno Rapée

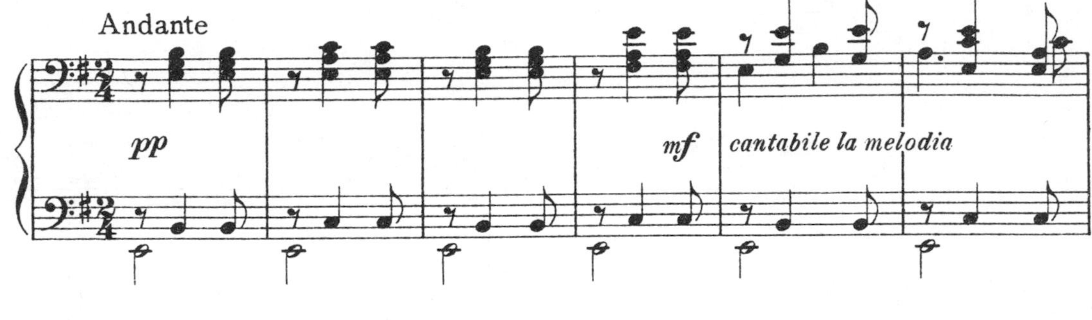

23377

pp
mf
l.h.
cresc.
poco rit.
f a tempo
p
Più moto
dolce
mf
p
pp

f affettuoso
mf
6
cresc.
molto
f
ff
dolente
p dolce
dim.
pp
ppp

Åse's Death

Edited and fingered by
Louis Oesterle

Edvard Grieg. Op. 46, No 2

ff
p
Ped. simile
più p
dim.
pp

Romance

Edited and fingered by
W. K. Bassford

A. Rubinstein. Op. 44, No. 1

cresc.
rit.
a tempo.
f
cresc.
f
f
p
8

Chanson Triste.

Edited and fingered by
W. K. Bassford

P. Tschaikowsky. Op. 40, No. 2

15801

f
p
poco rit.
p a tempo
f
p
mf
p
pp
ppp

Album-leaf

L. Birkedal Barfod
from Op. 7

agitato
mf
f
rit.
a tempo
p
molto rit.
a tempo
pp
a tempo
rit.
a tempo
f
rit.
a tempo
p
cresc.
rit.
morendo
pp

23731
31381

Andante Patetico e Doloroso

For deep sorrow, sickness or death

Gaston Borch

Più moto
p
cresc.
p
cresc.
f
ff
allarg.
p
p
Tempo Iº
cresc.
poco accel.
f
mf
mf
f
poco allarg.
rall. e dim.
ppp

Pathetic Andante No.1

(Depicting Sadness, Sorrow, *etc.*)

Herzwunden

Heart-sores

Edvard Grieg. Op. 34, No. 1

Allegretto espressivo.

cresc.

cresc.

cresc. molto

la melodia molto cantabile

15543

cresc.
pp
cresc. molto
f
fp
r.h.
l.h.
pp
f marcato
fz
più f
cresc.
molto
dimin. e rit.
pp

Mélodie

Élégie

Edited and fingered by
Louis Oesterle

Jules Massenet. Op. 10

Lento, ma non troppo

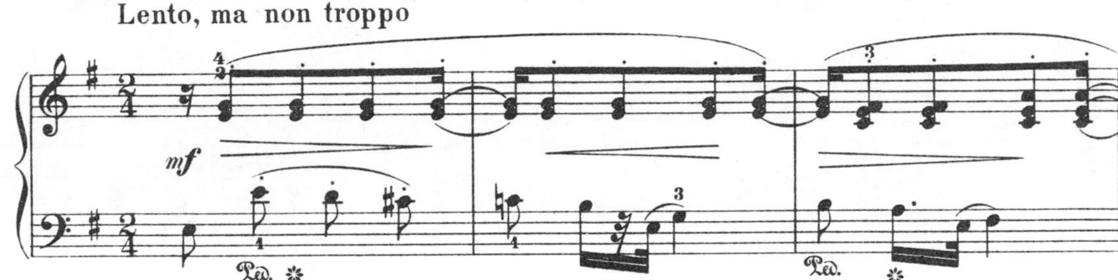

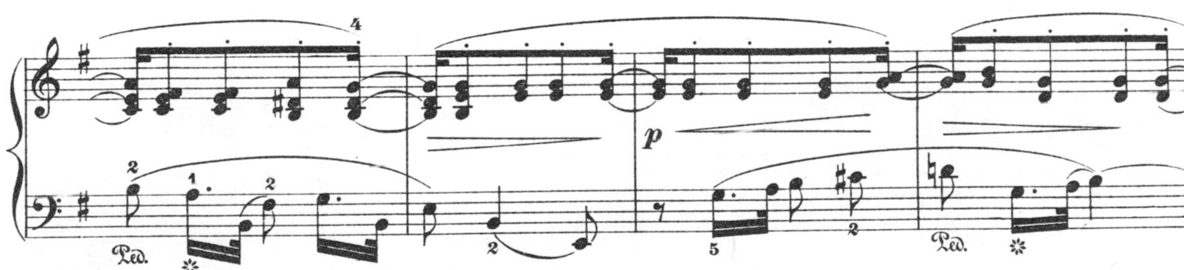

a tempo.
riten.
mf
Ped.
cresc.
p dim.
pp riten.
a tempo
f
più lento
dim.
molto più lento a capriccio
l. h.

In der Halle des Bergkönigs

In the Hall of the Mountain King

Edited and fingered by
Louis Oesterle

Alla marcia e molto marcato. (♩ = 138)

Edvard Grieg. Op. 46, No. 4

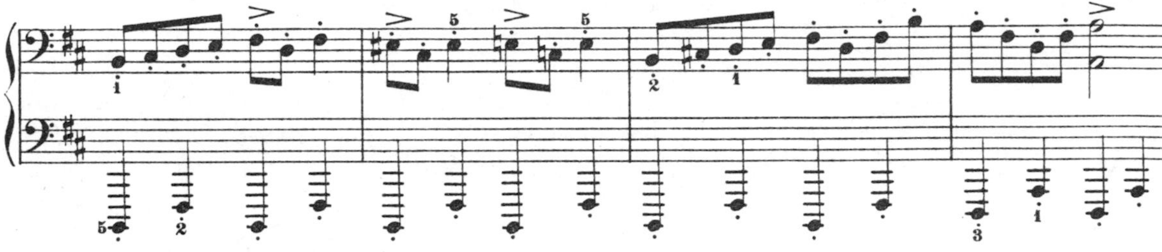

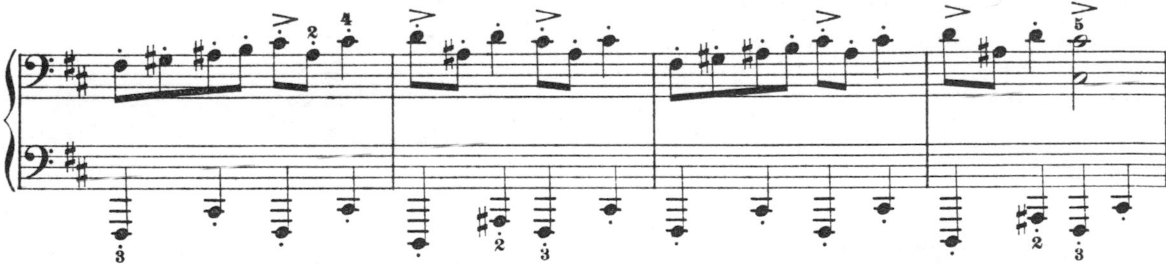

16249 r
14922

p
poco a poco cresc. e stretto

mf
e sempre cresc.
ff più vivo
sempre stretto al fine
Ped.

fz
pp
cresc. molto
p
ff
Ped.

Peer Gynt's Homecoming

Stormy evening on the coast

Edvard Grieg

Allegro molto agitato

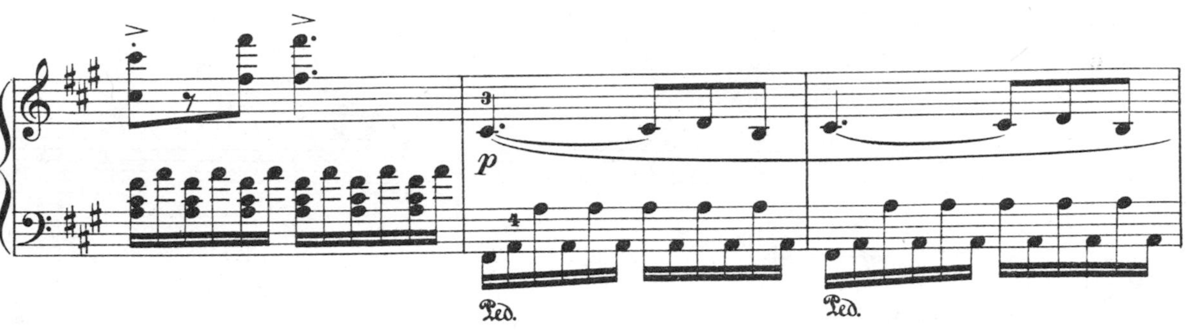

Ped.

dim.
pp
Ped.
Ped.
pp
Ped.

pp
Ped.
Ped.
cresc.
Ped.
Ped.
Ped.

dim.
Ped.
p
Ped.
ff
Ped.
p
f
Ped.
p
dim.
fp
fp
Ped.
fp
fp

f
fp
Ped.
fz

29690
81381

pp
ff
Ped.
fz
fp
D. C.

Coriolan
Overture

L. van Beethoven

Allegro con brio

31381

p
fz
fz cresc.
ff
fz
D. C.

Western Allegro

For joyful scenes, racing, stampedes, crowds, *etc.*

Edward Falck

28304

Western Allegro

For Western Scenes: Camping, mining, cowboys, stampedes, bar-rooms, gambling houses, *etc.*

Hugo Riesenfeld

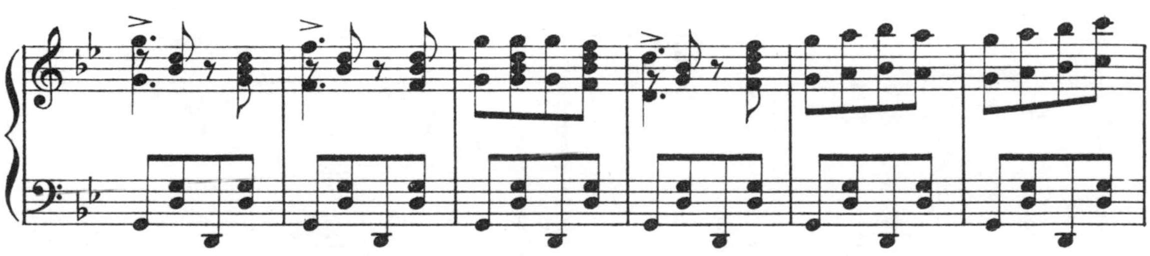

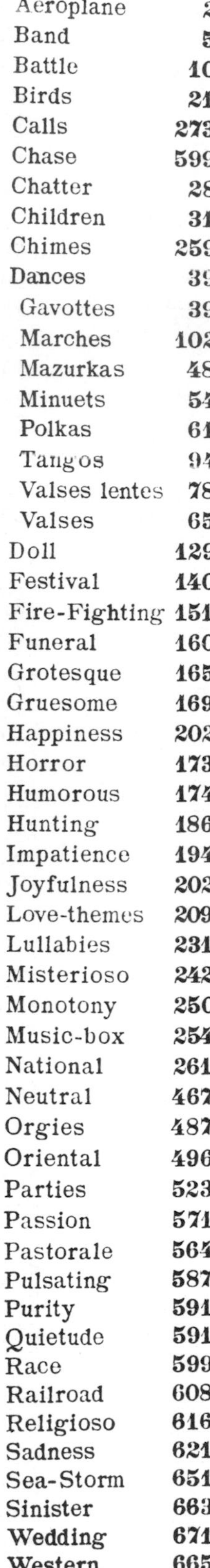

Fine

f *p* *f* *p*

1.

2.

f

D.S. al Fine

Western Scene

For animated Crowd Scenes, Fast Riding and Chasing, Cowboy gatherings, *etc.*

Irénée Bergé

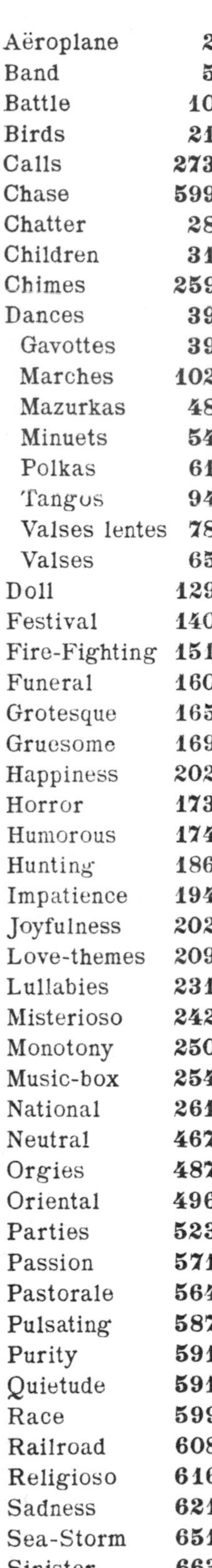

D.S. al Fine

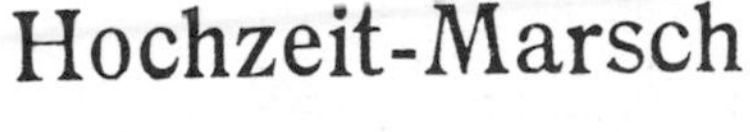

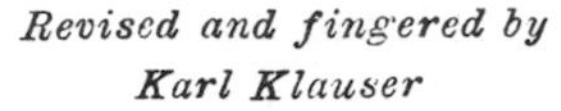
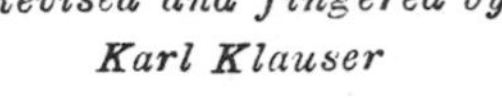

F. Mendelssohn

Allegro vivace.

Printed in the U. S. A.

Aëroplane 2
Band 5
Battle 10
Birds 21
Calls 273
Chase 599
Chatter 28
Children 31
Chimes 259
Dances 39
Gavottes 39
Marches 102
Mazurkas 48
Minuets 54
Polkas 61
Tangos 94
Valses lentes 78
Valses 65
Doll 129
Festival 140
Fire-Fighting 151
Funeral 160
Grotesque 165
Gruesome 169
Happiness 202
Horror 173
Humorous 174
Hunting 186
Impatience 194
Joyfulness 202
Love-themes 209
Lullabies 231
Misterioso 242
Monotony 250
Music-box 254
National 261
Neutral 467
Orgies 487
Oriental 496
Parties 523
Passion 571
Pastorale 564
Pulsating 587
Purity 591
Quietude 591
Race 599
Railroad 608
Religioso 616
Sadness 621
Sea-Storm 651
Sinister 663
Wedding 671
Western 665
672
Hochzeit-Marsch
Wedding March
from "Lohengrin"
Arranged by E. Pauer
Richard Wagner
Con moto moderato.
p
mf
p
p
legato.
p
Ped. * Ped. *
Ped. *
D. C.
(to measure 5)
31381

673
"O promise me"
Song
Reginald de Koven
Excerpt from Transcription for Piano by
James H. Rogers
dolce tranquillo
p
Ped.
poco accel.
rallent.
Moderato.
ben cantando
Aëroplane 2
Band 5
Battle 10
Birds 21
Calls 273
Chase 599
Chatter 28
Children 31
Chimes 259
Dances 39
Gavottes 39
Marches 102
Mazurkas 48
Minuets 54
Polkas 61
Tangos 94
Valses lentes 78
Valses 65
Doll 129
Festival 140
Fire-Fighting 151
Funeral 160
Grotesque 165
Gruesome 169
Happiness 202
Horror 173
Humorous 174
Hunting 186
Impatience 194
Joyfulness 202
Love-themes 209
Lullabies 231
Misterioso 242
Monotony 250
Music-box 254
National 261
Neutral 467
Orgies 487
Oriental 496
Parties 523
Passion 571
Pastorale 564
Pulsating 587
Purity 591
Quietude 591
Race 599
Railroad 608
Religioso 616
Sadness 621
Sea-Storm 651
Sinister 663
Wedding 671
Western 665

p semplice
poco rall.
p con tenerezza
dolce marc. la melodia
cresc.
sempre cresc.
f rall.
dim.
p
pesante
f
mp D. C.

INDEX

PAGE

Abduction of the Bride (Peer Gynt Suite): Grieg 173
Adagio (3rd movement l'Arlésienne Suite): Bizet 591
Adeste Fideles: Reading 301
Adjutant's Call: Tomlinson 275
Agitato No. 2: Andino 153
Agitato No. 3: Langey 10
Agitato misterioso: Langey 246
A la Polka: Fibich 206
Albumblatt (Album-leaf): Grieg 474
Album-leaf: Birkedal-Barfod 642
Alice, where art thou?: Ascher 307
Allegro No. 1: Minot 599
Allegro di molto e con brio: Beethoven 17
Allegro misterioso: Langey 246
Allegro misterioso notturno: Borch 244
Alma Mater: Shepard 289
America (My country, 'tis of thee): Carey 262
Among the Arabs: Langey 496
Andante molto sostenuto (*Phèdre*): Massenet 173
Andante patetico e doloroso: Borch 644
Andante pathétique No. 1: Schumann 161
An den Frühling (To Spring): Grieg 582
Annie Laurie 441
April Smile: Depret 83
Arab Dance: Grieg 510
Arabesque: Wrangell 476
Argentine National Hymn (Oid, mortales, el grito sagrado) 311
Arlésienne Suite (Pastorale): Bizet 570
Arlésienne Suite (1st movement): Bizet 519
Arlésienne Suite (3rd movement): Bizet 591
Arlésienne Suite (4th movement): Bizet 487
Ase's Death: Grieg 636
Assembly March: Tomlinson 277
Attack by the Uhlans: Bohm 108
Auf freiem Fusse: Strauss 63
Auld Lang Syne 439
Australian Patriotic Air (There is a land where summer skies) 314
Austrian Patriotic Air (O du mein Österreich) 315
Autumn and Winter (L'Automne et l'Hiver): Glazounoff 494

Bådnlåt (Cradle-song): Grieg 252
Bajadère, Die: Strauss 603
Ballet-Suite (*Salammbô*): Arends 159
Ballroom Whispers: Gregh 88
Barcarolle (*Tales of Hoffmann*): Offenbach 398
Battle-Cry of Freedom, The: Root 265
Battle Hymn of the Republic: Root 267
Bayamesa, La (Cuban National Song) 327
Belgian National Hymn (La Brabançonne) 317
Berceuse: Grieg 235
Berceuse (Lullaby): Iljinsky 231
Berceuse: Järnefelt 633

PAGE

Birdling (Vöglein): Grieg 26
Birds: Wright 21
Bluebells of Scotland 440
Bohemia (Patriotic Air) 316
Brabançonne, La (Belgian National Hymn) 317
Brazilian Maxixe-Tango (Dengozo): Nazareth 94
Brazilian National Hymn 318
Bulgarian National Hymn 319
Butterfly (Papillon): Grieg 23

Campbells are Coming, The 440
Caprice (Vanity): Jackson 523
Card Trio (*Carmen*): Bizet 157
Carillon, Le (4th movement l'Arlésienne Suite): Bizet 568
Cascaden-Galop: Herrmann 605
Cavatina: Raff 219
Chanson Triste: Tschaikowsky 640
Chant d'Amour (Love-Song): Paderewski 229
Chant du Départ 351
Chant sans Paroles: Friml 485
Chant sans Paroles (Song without Words): Tschaikowsky 557
Children's Dance: Noble 36
Chilean National Song (Dulce Patria) 322
Chinese-Japanese: Langey 331
Chinese Lullaby: Bowers 338
Chinese National Hymn 324, 330
Cinquantaine, La: Gabriel-Marie 129
College Hornpipe 382
College Songs March: Shepard 285
Columbian National Hymn 324
Columbia, the Gem of the Ocean—The Red, White and Blue 264
Comin' Through the Rye 443
Coriolan (Overture): Beethoven 663
Coronation March: Meyerbeer 144
Cossack Lullaby (Kosácka ukolébavka): Jiránek 429
Costa Rican National Song (De la Patria) 326
Coucou, Le: Arensky 183
Cradle-Song (Bådnlåt): Grieg 252
Cuban National Song (La Bayamesa) 327
Curious Story: Keller 178
Czarina, La: Ganne 48

Dance from Jölster: Grieg 169
Dance of the Young Maidens: Strickland 377
Danish National Hymn 344
Danse Polonaise (Krakowiak): Mlynarski 420
Danza (Nos. 1 and 2: Six Cuban Dances) 328
De la Patria (Costa Rican National Song) 326
Dengozo (Brazilian): Nazareth 94
Dickory, dickory, dock 31
Die Bajadère: Strauss 603
Die Mühle (The Mill): Jensen 608

	Page
Die Wacht am Rhein	353
Ding dong bell	31
Dios salve a Honduras	357
Dixie-Land : Emmet	281
Drink to me only with thine eyes	346
Dulce Patria (Chilean National Song)	322
Dutch National Hymn (Mijn Neêrlandsch Bloed)	356
Élégie : Grieg	631
Élégie (Mélodie) : Massenet	649
Erl-King, The (Le Roi des Aulnes) : Schubert	248
Estudiantina Valses : Waldteufel	455
Eventide (Le Soir) : Schytte	592
Exhibition March : Fahrbach	102
Fair Flatterer, The : Eilenberg	43
Fair Harvard	290
Faith (Song without words) : Mendelssohn	594
Fanfare e Marcia Reale (Italy)	386
First Movement l'Arlésienne Suite : Bizet	519
First Movement l'Arlésienne Suite No. 2 (Pastorale) : Bizet	570
First Movement Sonata, Op. 13 : Beethoven	17
First Movement Sonata, Quasi una Fantasia, Op. 27, No. 2 : Beethoven	625
Fisher's Hornpipe	382
Fourth Movement l'Arlésienne Suite : Bizet	487
Fourth Movement l'Arlésienne Suite (Le Carillon) : Bizet	568
Friedrichs-Marsch : Gungl	114
Fuji-Ko (Japanese Intermezzo) : Shelley	340
Funeral March (Song without Words) : Mendelssohn	163
Furioso No. 3 : Langey	155
Galop (Die Bajadère) : Strauss	603
Galop (Leichtes Blut) : Strauss	601
Garibaldi Hymn	389
Garry Owen	381
Gaudeamus	290
Gavotte from Mignon : Thomas	39
General's March, The : Tomlinson	276
German Patrol, The : Eilenberg	5
Gloria al bravo Pueblo (Venezuelan National Hymn)	465
God Save the King: Carey	345
Golandrina, La (Mexican National Song)	406
Golden Wedding, The : Gabriel-Marie	129
Grecian National Hymn	354
Hail Columbia	262
Happy Wanderer : Jensen	202
Hark! The Herald Angels Sing : Mendelssohn	300
Hawaii pouoi (National Hymn)	352

	Page
Herzwunden (Heart-Sores) : Grieg	647
Hey diddle diddle	32
Himno de Riego (Spanish National Hymn)	446
Hochzeit-Marsch (Wedding March) : Mendelssohn	671
Hochzeit-Marsch (Wedding March) (*Lohengrin*) : Wagner	672
Holy Night : Gruber	302
Homeless (Song without Words) : Mendelssohn	199, 579
Home, Sweet Home : Bishop	304
Honduras National Hymn (Dios salve a Honduras)	357
Humoreske : Grieg	180
Humoresque : Tschaikowsky	174
Humoristic Dance (Stabbe-Laaten) : Grieg	181
Humpty Dumpty	33
Hungarian National Song	358
Hunter's Call : Reinhold	190
Hunter's Horn, The : Schmoll	192
Hunting Song : Schumann	186, 191
Hurry No. 2 : Langey	151
Hymn of Free Russia (Gimn svobodnoi Rossii) : Gretchaninoff	425
Idilio : Lack	527
Idylle aus der Hochzeit zu Wulfsberg : Söderman	416
Impatience (Song without Words) : Gregh	194
In a Chinese Tea-room : Langey	333
In der Halle des Bergkönigs (In the Hall of the Mountain King): Grieg	651
Indian Agitato : Langey	367
Indian War-dance : Bergé	369
Indian War-dance : Borch	371
In Sight of the Oasis (Vers l'Oasis) : Baron	506
In the Hall of the Mountain King (In der Halle des Bergkönigs) : Grieg	651
Italian National Hymn (Fanfare e Marcia Reale)	386
Jack and Jill	34
Jagd-Fanfare : Reinhold	190
Jagdlied : Schumann	186
Jägerliedchen : Schumann	191
Japanese National Hymn (Kimygayo)	330
Jingle Bells	299
Juanita (Spanish Ballad)	453
Killarney	383
Kimygayo (Japanese National Hymn)	330
Klokkeklang (Ringing Bells): Grieg	259
Kosácka ukolébavka (Cossack Lullaby) : Jiránek	429
Krakowiak (Polonaise) : Mlynarski	420
Kuriose Geschichte : Heller	178

PAGE

Ladies' Faces, Ribbons and Laces : Wyatt 550
Largo : Händel 616
Last Movement Sonata, Op. 10, No. 2 : Beethoven 28
L'Automne et l'Hiver (Autumn and Winter): Glazounoff 494
Lead, Kindly Light : Sullivan 620
Leichtes Blut (Galop) : Strauss 601
Listen to the Mocking-bird : Hawthorne 309
Lost Happiness (Song without Words) : Mendelssohn 577
Lotus Lake, The : Dutton 471
Love's Greeting (Salut d'Amour) : Elgar 560
Love's Old, Sweet Song : Molloy 305
Love-Song : Friml 223
Love-Song (Chant d'Amour) : Paderewski 229
Lullaby : Wright 233
Lullaby (Berceuse) : Iljinsky 231

Maple-leaf for ever (Canadian) 320
March and Procession of Bacchus (*Sylvia*) : Delibes 148
Marche Funèbre : Chopin 160
Marche Héroïque : Schubert 140
March of the Dwarfs (Zug der Zwerge) : Grieg 242
Marcia (Portuguese National Hymn) 423
Maria, Marì! : Di Capua 391
Marseillaise, La 349
Mary had a little lamb 35
Mazurka : Dutton 51
Mélodie (Élégie) : Massenet 649
Melody : Rubinstein 226
Men of Harlech (Welsh National Song) 466
Mexican National Song (La Golandrina) 406
Mignon (Gavotte) : Thomas 39
Mijn Neêrlandsch Bloed (Dutch National Hymn) 356
Mill, The (Die Mühle) : Jensen 608
Minuet (from Sonata Op. 49, No. 2) : Beethoven 54
Minuet : Boccherini 58
Misterioso No. 1 : Langey 165
Misterioso No. 2 : Minot 171
Misterioso Infernale : Borch 169
Moment Musical No. 1 : Schubert 479
Moment Musical No. 2 : Schubert 483
Monte Cristo : Kotlar 78
Morgenstimmung (Morning Mood) : Grieg 564
Morris Dance : Noble 501
Mourir pour la Patrie 352
Music-Box : Friml 254
My Old Kentucky Home : Foster 282
My Sunshine ('O Sole mio) : Di Capua 394

Nancy Lee : Adams 292
Norwegian Dance : Grieg 413

PAGE

Norwegian National Song (Sönner af Norge) 408
Norwegisch (Norwegian Melody) : Grieg 411

O du mein Österreich (Austrian Patriotic Air) 315
Oid, mortales, el grito sagrado (Argentine National Hymn) 311
Old Folks at Home (Swanee River): Foster 283
Old Hundredth, The : Bourgeois 619
Old Mother, The : Dvořák 209
Oloha, oe (Hawaii) 355
Onward, Christian Soldiers : Sullivan 619
O Promise Me : De Koven 673
'O Sole mio (My Sunshine): Di Capua 394
Overture to Phèdre: Massenet 173

Papillon (Butterfly) : Grieg 23
Partant pour la Syrie 350
Pastorale (1st movement l'Arlésienne Suite No. 2) : Bizet 570
Pathetic Andante No. 1 : Langey 646
Peer Gynt's Home-coming (Stormy Evening on the Coast) : Grieg 655
Pizzicati (from *Sylvia*) : Delibes 538
Plantation Melody : Farwell 284
Poem: Fibich 217
Poland's not yet dead in slavery (Patriotic Air) 419
Portuguese National Hymn (Marcia) 423
Poupée Valsante : Poldini 134
Prelude : Chopin (Op. 28, No. 4) 629
Prelude : Chopin (Op. 28, No. 20) 630
Presto (Sonata Op. 10, No. 2) : Beethoven 28
Presto agitato (Moonlight Sonata) : Beethoven 13

Radiance : Sellars 467
Rákóczy March (Hungarian) 359
Red, White and Blue, The—Columbia, the Gem of the Ocean 264
Repose (Song without Words) : Gregh 587
Reveille : Tomlinson 273
Rheinland Regiment March : Král 126
Ringing Bells (Klokkeklang) : Grieg 259
Robin Adair 306
Rocked in the Cradle of the Deep : Knight 295
Roi des Aulnes, Le (The Erl-King) : Schubert 248
Romance : Frommel 621
Romance : Rubinstein 638
Romance : Williams 211
Rondo Capriccioso : Mendelssohn 2
Roumanian National Hymn (Traesca Regele) 424
Rule, Britannia 345
Russian Dance : Friml 431

Saint Patrick's Day 385
Salammbô (Ballet-Suite) : Arends 159
Sally in Our Alley : Carey 303

PAGE

Salut d'Amour (Love's Greeting) : Elgar 560
Scarf Dance (Scène de Ballet) : Chaminade 530
Scherzo : Mendelssohn 3
Scots, wha hae wi' Wallace bled 442
Serbian National Anthem (Srpska Narodna Himna) 444
Serenade : Olsen 597
Serenade : Sokolowski 238
Sérénade Badine : Gabriel-Marie 542
Serenata : Moszkowski 547
Sirènes, Les : Waldteufel 71
Slavic Dance : Dvořák 361
Soir, Le (Eventide) : Schytte 592
Song without Words (Chant sans paroles) : Tschaikowsky 557
Song without Words (Faith) : Mendelssohn 594
Song without Words (Funeral March) : Mendelssohn 163
Song without Words (Homeless) : Mendelssohn 199, 579
Song without Words (Impatience) : Gregh 194
Song without Words (Lost Happiness) : Mendelssohn 577
Song without Words (Repose) : Gregh 587
Song without Words (Spring Song) : Mendelssohn 553
Song without Words (Tarantella) : Mendelssohn 29
Song without Words (Venetian Boat-Song) : Mendelssohn 396
Sönner af Norge (Norwegian National Song) 408
Southwestern Idyl : Bergé 279
Souvenir : Drdla 533
Spanish Dance No. 1 : Moszkowski 447
Spanish Dance No. 2 : Moszkowski 450
Spanish National Hymn (Himno de Riego) 446
Spinning-Song (*Flying Dutchman*) : Wagner 612
Spring Song (Song without Words) : Mendelssohn 553
Srpska Narodna Himna (Serbian National Anthem) 444
Stabbe-Laaten : Grieg 181
Standard-Bearer March : Fahrbach 105
Star-spangled Banner : Smith 261
Stimmt an mit hellem, hohen Klang 353
Stormy Evening on the Coast (Peer Gynt's Homecoming) : Grieg 655
Sun-Dance : Strickland 373
Swanee River (Old Folks at Home) : Foster 285
Swedish Wedding March : Söderman 416
Sylvia Ballet (Pizzicati) : Delibes 538

Tales of the Vienna Wood : Strauss 65
Tango Argentino (Y... ¿Como le vá?) : Valverde 98
Tanz aus Jölster : Grieg 167
Taps : Tomlinson 274

PAGE

Tarentelle : Lack 400
There is a land where summer skies (Australian Patriotic Air) 314
Third Movement l'Arlésienne Suite (Adagio) : Bizet 591
Third Movement Moonlight Sonata : Beethoven 13
To Spring (An den Frühling) : Grieg 582
To the Colors : Tomlinson 277
Traesca Regele (Roumanian National Hymn) 424
Tramp! tramp! tramp! : Root 269
Träumerei : Schumann 596

Une Tabatière à Musique (Valse-Badinage) : Liadow 257
Untiring Search : Stiehl 197
Upidee 291
Uruguayan National Hymn 463

Valse : Brahms 215
Valse-Badinage (Une Tabatière à Musique) : Liadow 257
Valzer appassionato : Dutton 571
Vanity (Caprice) : Jackson 523
Venetian Boat-Song (Song without Words) : Mendelssohn 396
Venezuelan National Hymn (Gloria al bravo Pueblo) 465
Vers l'Oasis (In Sight of the Oasis) : Baron 506
Vienna March : Schrammel 120
Vive la Canadienne 321
Vöglein (Birdling) : Grieg 26

Walzer : Grieg 409
Wacht am Rhein 353
Wearing o' the Green 384
Wedding March (Hochzeit-Marsch) : Mendelssohn 671
Wedding March (Hochzeit-Marsch *Lohengrin*) : Wagner 672
Wedding March (Swedish) : Söderman 416
Welsh National Song (Men of Harlech) 466
Western Allegro : Falck 665
Western Allegro : Riesenfeld 667
Western Scene : Bergé 669
We won't go home till morning 291
When you and I were young, Maggie : Butterfield 310
Wildfeuer : Joh. Strauss 61
With the Military : Fahrbach 117

Yankee Doodle 271
Y... ¿Como le va? (Tango Argentino) : Valverde 98

Zug der Zwerge (March of the Dwarfs) : Grieg 242